MANY WAYS UP

MANY WAYS UP

A Bullying and Mental Health Workbook

COPE

DEAL

HEAL

CHANGE

Making a Difference:
A Discussion Guide for the Novel, THE ONLY WAY OUT

KATIE KUPERMAN

Many Ways Up: A Bullying and Mental Health Workbook

Copyright © 2023 by Katie Kuperman

All rights reserved. No part of this book may be reproduced or transmitted in any form or by any means, electronic or mechanical, including photocopying, recording, or by any information storage and retrieval system without the written permission of the author, except where permitted by law.

The story, all names, characters, and incidents portrayed in this production are fictitious. No identification with actual persons (living or deceased), places, buildings, and products is intended or should be inferred.

This publication is designed to provide accurate and authoritative information in regard to the subject matter covered. It is sold with the understanding that neither the author nor the publisher is engaged in rendering legal, investment, accounting or other professional services. While the publisher and author have used their best efforts in preparing this book, they make no representations or warranties with respect to the accuracy or completeness of the contents of this book and specifically disclaim any implied warranties of merchantability or fitness for a particular purpose. No warranty may be created or extended by sales representatives or written sales materials. The advice and strategies contained herein may not be suitable for your situation. You should consult with a professional when appropriate. Neither the publisher nor the author shall be liable for any loss of profit or any other commercial damages, including but not limited to special, incidental, consequential, personal, or other damages.

Print ISBN 978-1-7388496-0-4
eBook ISBN 978-1-7388496-1-1

TABLE OF CONTENTS

Foreword ix

1. The Act of Bullying 1
    Discussion Questions 2
    Things to Think About 3
    What is a Bully? 4
    People Who Bully 4
    Moving Forward 6
    Actionable Tasks 7

2. The Victimized 13
    Discussion Questions 15
    Things to Think About 16
    What is a Victim? 17
    People Who Are Victimized 17
    Why Was I Victimized? 17
    Moving Forward 18
    Actionable Tasks 20

3. The Bystander 29
    Discussion Questions 31
    Things to Think About 32
    What is a Bystander? 33
    People Who Are Bystanders 33
    Imagine 34
    Wrong Place, Wrong Time 36

    Have a Responsibility..36
    Moving Forward..36
    Silence or Action?..37
    Actionable tasks...37

4. Social Media and Cyberbullying..43
    Discussion Questions..44
    Things to Think About..45
    What is Cyberbullying?..46
    Impact on Mental Health and Wellbeing...................47
    Managing and Limiting Time.......................................48
    Moving Forward..49
    Actionable Tasks..50

5. Friendship..55
    The Value of Friendships..56
    The Beauties and the Complexities............................57
    Loyalty and Betrayal...57
    Discussion Questions..58
    Things to Think About..59
    Moving Forward..60
    Actionable Tasks..61

6. Self-Confidence..65
    Discussion Questions..66
    Things to Think About..67
    The "Act" of Confidence...68
    Exuding Confidence—Even When We Don't *Feel* Confident................69
    Being Our Authentic Selves...70
    Choosing Where We Want to Be..................................73
    We're Worth It..73
    Moving Forward..74
    Actionable Tasks..75

7. Dealing with the Aftermath..81
    Discussion Questions..83
    Things to Think About..84

  When Something Happens 84
  Go Through the Motions 85
  Moving Forward 86
  Actionable Tasks 86

8. Support Crew 91
  Discussion Questions 92
  Things to Think About 93
  What is a Support Network? 94
  Why Do We Need a Support Network? 94
  What if We Don't Have a Network? 95
  Moving Forward 95
  Actionable Tasks 96

9. All the Ways Up Start with Talking 101
  Discussion Questions 103
  Things to Think About 104
  Why Talk? 104
  Talking to Someone Who Needs Help 106
  Talking to Someone When *You* Need Help 106
  Moving Forward 107
  Actionable Tasks 108

10. Making a Change 113
  Discussion Questions 115
  Things to Think About 115
  Perspective and Perception 116
  Rewind, Be Kind 116
  Be Kind to *Yourself* 119
  We Can 120
  Moving Forward 122
  Actionable Tasks 123

Help Resources 128

References 129

FOREWORD

If there is one comment I hear consistently from people who have read my debut novel, *The Only Way Out*, it is this: "You made me feel something."

Some have stated the story brought them to tears. For several adult readers, it took them back to their high school years with a diverse collection of memories. Others, who have known loss, expressed that the story once again brought to the forefront those intense feelings related to their tragedy. What all of these have in common is the testimony that the novel touched them in some meaningful way.

Such responses have been gratifying beyond words. When I wrote *The Only Way Out*, the task I assigned myself was to draw attention to two serious issues faced by our young people today. I weaved a story that seeks to raise awareness about bullying and mental health in a manner that neither the heart nor the brain can ignore. To hear that many of my readers have felt about the book exactly as I wished them to, is a reward like no other.

When we are processing past events or trying to find better ways of learning from difficult situations, first we must *feel*. Those feelings may be a result of what we've read, what we've seen, what we've done or what we've experienced. Once we have a strong feeling or emotion, this creates a path that leads us to *learn and process*. Here's when we raise our level of awareness, educate ourselves and seek to answer the questions we have. Then, comes action. When we understand what we felt, why we felt it, how it ties into our daily lives, and the next steps we can take in a positive direction, it's time to *do*.

As the philosophers remind us:

> We are not judged by what we think or say, but rather by what we do.

Now, here I sit, celebrating the one-year anniversary of my release of *The Only Way Out*. The book received media coverage on television, landed news article features, earned me guest spots on podcasts, and attracted the attention of schools, principals and teachers in the educational space. Since the book's launch, I cannot begin to tell you how incredible it has been to share my emotional story with the world and to have such positive and encouraging feedback. When the dust began to settle slightly, I found myself asking an important question: *what next?*

Eventually, the answer to that question became crystal clear.

This book is next. The very one you're about to experience.

WHAT IS IT?

Many Ways Up is not your run-of-the-mill nonfiction book, nor is it a typical classroom workbook. It is something in between. Something unique. Something accessible. Something that allows for the processing of information and feelings in real, concrete ways so we may work through them and use them to our advantage moving forward.

This is an accompaniment to my novel, and it is my goal and intention that the two pieces can serve as a "package" and "mini unit" on bullying and mental health for teachers, educators, counselors, parents, youth and young adults who want to advance the conversation and create change.

Foreword

It is a nonfiction, narrative, workbook and teaching resource designed to help us raise our awareness around bullying and mental health, deepen our understanding of these issues, gain fresh perspectives within our own lives and the lives of others, and learn ways to move forward with actionable steps that make a positive difference.

Many Ways Up dissects 10 different elements (presented in the form of sections) of bullying and mental health struggles that are addressed in *The Only Way Out*. Every section includes discussion questions for in-class environments, educational components for knowledge building, tips for moving forward and a list of actionable tasks inclusive of visual and written exercises for solution-focused next steps.

I've created the content with the following objectives:

- Be accessible
- Open doors to fresh perspectives and new ideas
- Present realistic solutions and steps forward
- Enable readers to gain insight and better understand themselves and others
- Create dialogue and discussion
- Break the silent cycle
- Encourage, inspire and motivate people to talk openly and speak up

I wrote *The Only Way Out* to evoke emotion and awareness.

I wrote *Many Ways Up* to take that emotion and awareness, and translate it into real-life applications and a collective movement towards meaningful, positive change.

The latter cannot come without the former.

First, we *feel*.
Then, we *learn*.
Finally, we *do*.

You'll also notice each section of the book ends with its own key message takeaway for these three critical components of FEEL, LEARN and DO.

TOGETHER IS *THE ONLY WAY OUT*

The world now refers to bullying and mental health as epidemics plaguing people on a global scale. These are no longer problems only a few people face.

- 1 out of 3 teens is bullied worldwide (UNESCO)
- 10% of children and adolescents experience a mental illness worldwide (WHO)
- Suicide is the 4th leading cause of death in 15-to-19-year-olds worldwide (WHO)

We are seeing widespread, alarmingly high rates of bullying and mental illness, particularly among youth and young adults, and the two issues often go hand in hand. Bullying can lead to negative mental health repercussions, and mental health struggles can lead to acts of bullying as well as the inability to cope with distressing situations.

We were put on this earth with a tremendous gift.

The gift of communication.

We are able to talk to one another. Make plans. Teach. Learn. Create laughter. Express our feelings. Get things off our chest. Ask a person for a favor. Tell someone where to go. Sometimes, even deciding not to respond and to turn the other way is an effective form of communication.

If we take a second to think about this gift, this human skill, it doesn't take long to realize how special it is. The unfortunate reality, however, is that we don't always use it. In fact, sometimes in the direst situations when we need to use it the most, we can't. We feel paralyzed. Trapped. Afraid.

"I can't say that—what will they think of me?"
"This is far too embarrassing. I need to keep this to myself."
"I'm in trouble, but no one will understand."
"I don't know how to talk about this."
"I have no idea where to start."

Foreword

We are all humans, living our lives together side by side. Whether we like to acknowledge our connection to one another or not, it's a fact. Your troubles aren't the same as his troubles, her troubles, their troubles or my troubles, but we all have them. There is no need to go it alone. You're on your journey and everyone else is on theirs, and yet we can learn from one another and appreciate each other's circumstances. Sometimes our willingness to be vulnerable makes others relate more—not less.

How many times have you read an article or watched a video where someone opened up about themselves and shared a piece of information that made you say, "Phew! I'm so relieved I'm not the only one." Or imagine a friend told you something in confidence and instantly you could relate to one another on a mutual struggle at a whole new level?

Communication creates connection.
Communication brings us together.

If we can foster a sense of togetherness instead of judgment and segregation, we can come to a point of regular, open and honest communication—no matter what the topic is. In the vast majority of cases, the biggest tragedies associated with bullying and mental health can be attributed to a lack of communication, silence, isolation and seclusion.

British Columbia teen, Amanda Todd, felt secluded from the friends she'd made and the world around her because of a relentless cyberbully and a series of events that all stemmed from one personal "mistake" online that haunted her until the day she died.

It was reported in many news outlets that Texas school shooter, Salvador Ramos, was bullied and over time this led to him gradually dropping out of school and adopting a more reclusive way of life with little to no communication with others.

Manitoba teenager, Daniel Lints, had everything going for him but after he was coerced into an explicit digital exchange, he chose silence and died by suicide.

A 12-year-old elementary school girl in Tokyo, Japan, took her own life after being bullied by her classmates on a chat app on the iPad she used at school. The girl's mother reported that she had no idea her daughter was bullied until after she killed herself.

What if these people felt accepted and loved for what they were going through?
What if they knew they had trusted people to turn to, talk to, and work through problems with?
What if the customary and encouraged protocol was to talk to someone right away, which would then guarantee them real and immediate help?
What if more people knew and helping hands were offered?
What if they didn't feel so alone?
What if they felt a strong sense of <u>togetherness</u>?

Would these tragedies still have happened?

It is my strong hope and vision that *Many Ways Up* may act as a step in a positive direction to help our young people of today build awareness, strengthen their minds, and always know that it's right to talk openly and speak up.

THE ACT OF BULLYING

We took the last few steps towards the cafeteria doors but were suddenly halted close to the opening. A rather large lineup had formed. I suppose everyone else had the same idea we did.

"Watch it!" the tall girl ahead of us snarled, looking directly at Rebecca.

"Sorry," Rebecca answered sheepishly, appearing quite stunned.

Despite the compassionate and apologetic nature of Rebecca's response, the girl continued to stare. Looking Rebecca up and down in a judgmental, condescending manner, the hateful stranger rolled her tongue over her teeth. After swiftly flashing an evil glance in my direction, she turned around to face the line in front of her.

Rebecca and I slowly turned our heads towards one another and shared a look of alarm. Rebecca's face was flush with embarrassment and my heartbeat quickened as my nerves escalated. As much as I could tell how badly we each wanted to exchange our take on the confusing encounter that had just taken place, we most certainly couldn't with her standing right in front of us! Thank goodness our awkward moment was masked by the hustle and bustle of the cafeteria.

~ **Chapter 3**, *The Only Way Out*

DISCUSSION QUESTIONS

TAKE A MOMENT
Gain a deeper understanding.

1. In this scene, is this an act of bullying towards Rebecca? Why or why not?

2. Do you think it's okay for "the tall girl" to act this way towards Rebecca? How did her actions, words and behaviors impact Rebecca?

------

3. Could Rebecca and Kaitlyn have acted differently here? If yes, how? What would that have looked like and how would the outcome have changed?

THINGS TO THINK ABOUT

Perception is everything.

1. For some, this altercation might be considered significant. To others, it might not have been given so much as a second thought. It is largely a matter of perception. How you perceive a situation is a major contributory factor to the way in which you decide to respond.

2. While it's good practice not to take things too seriously, never hesitate when it comes to your own self-worth and safety. You deserve to be treated fairly and with respect. This is your right.

3. Heighten your awareness. Be conscious of what happens *to* you and *around* you. Evaluate situations to the best of your ability. If you believe action is required, handle it immediately, in the way you are most comfortable and think will be most effective.

WHAT IS A BULLY?

A bully can be defined as a person who continually seeks to harm, intimidate or coerce people they perceive as vulnerable. The repetition and deliberate targeting of those with "less power" is what separates *bullying* from run-of-the-mill *aggression*.

Instead of focusing on what a bully is, however, let us refocus on the *act of bullying.* It isn't wise, fair or accurate simply to label people. A person who engages in bullying behavior, is not a "bully."

Why not?

Because they have the ability to stop that behavior. There is an opportunity for change, and we cannot discount that nor discourage it.

PEOPLE WHO BULLY

> A healthy mind does not speak ill of others.

Bullying doesn't simply happen out of nowhere and for no reason. It is the result of some prior issue, challenge or unaddressed situation. For example, it can arise after trauma, problems at home, peer pressure, low self-esteem or self-adjustment and mental health struggles.

There are no excuses for bullying, however, it is a worthwhile exercise to take a look at possible underlying factors so that we may better understand why people engage in bullying behaviors.

Psychologists state that people bully as a means to get what they want or to establish dominance (at least in the short term), and because they lack the social skills to do this without harming others.

1. The Act of Bullying

Research finds that those who engage in bullying behavior:

- Are not "prosocial" (positive, helpful, promoting friendship and social acceptance)
- Do not understand others' feelings
- Tend to be paranoid (misreading the intentions of others, inserting hostility in non-hostile situations)
- Often have strained relationships with peers and parents
- Suffer from low self-esteem

According to BetterHelp, an online mental health platform offering licensed services to consumers, there can be many reasons *why* people bully, but a few are most common.

Take a look:

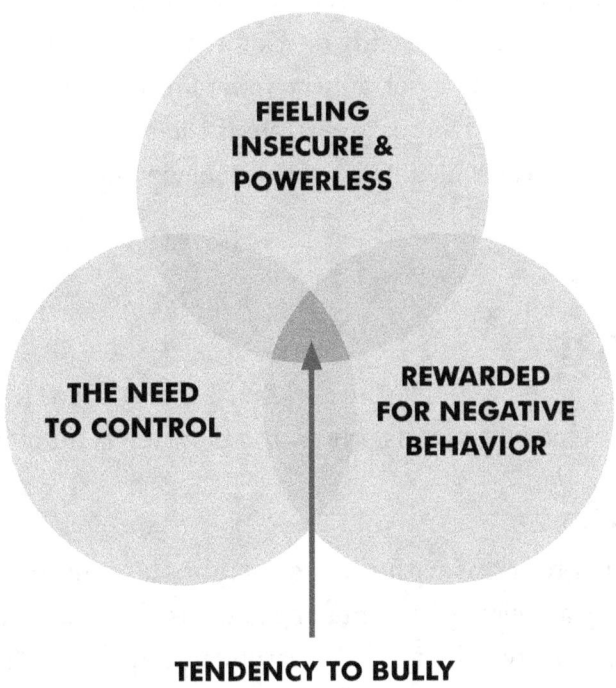

We have a tendency for bullying to take place when three elements converge and exist together:

1. Feelings of insecurity and powerlessness
2. The need to control
3. Being rewarded for negative behaviors

This further illustrates why it is so important for feelings to be openly expressed. When they are, these feelings can be understood and then subsequently addressed in an efficient and effective manner. If an act of bullying takes place, it is critical that we take a stand to prevent control, create a support group around us, stay neutral with our emotions to show they do not have power, and deal with it quickly so bad behaviors are not rewarded and it does not become a repetitive event.

Bullying is wrong and we cannot excuse people for treating others in this way. What we can do, however, is attempt to comprehend *why* it is happening. Putting ourselves in someone else's shoes is a simple exercise that can give us fresh insights. If we can even partially understand where someone else is coming from, what they are feeling or what they are going through, then we can have a more humanistic response. This will not only be more productive, but it will also reestablish a sense of togetherness instead of further segregation. If the person doing the bullying is understood and helped, there is a greater likelihood of the behavior stopping as opposed to persisting and causing further damage.

MOVING FORWARD

If we engage in bullying behavior towards others, the first step is full, nonjudgmental acknowledgement. *"Yes, I am doing this."*

The second step is coming to terms with the fact that because our behaviors negatively affect ourselves and others, they are wrong and must be addressed. We all make mistakes and we all have the ability to make positive changes, outwardly and inwardly. *"I did something wrong, I know it was wrong, so what will I do differently next time?"*

The third step is figuring out the WHY behind our actions. Why did we bully? It's time to tap into our emotions, run towards our feelings (not away from them) and start unraveling the core, root reason for lashing out. If we can find this, identify it and then deal with it effectively, we can see positive changes within ourselves.

The fourth step is getting help. Maybe that looks like an open conversation with a friend we can confide in. Or maybe we tell a loved one what we're going through. Or, perhaps it's on a professional level with a therapist. There's no shame here. We're all fighting battles of one kind or another. It's up to us to get the support, love, guidance and togetherness we need.

The fifth step is putting it all into action. Acknowledge, accept, understand, manage, change. Deeper understanding and new perspectives that let us truly comprehend what is happening inside of us, which further fuel our actions, are what ultimately set us free. Maybe we thought freedom would come by putting others down so we could be lifted up. Perhaps we simply didn't know any better, or we didn't yet have the awareness and skills to get what we needed a different way. It is possible to lift ourselves up higher by feeling empowered through a deeper understanding of who we are, what we care about, what drives us and how we want to be in the world. All of this then gets translated into everyday actions that treat both ourselves and others fairly, and create genuine happiness.

ACTIONABLE TASKS

1. Self reflect.

Do a ten-second personal check-in every day. Before you go to bed, evaluate how you felt about the day that is now just about finished. There are only three symbols to choose from to keep this quick and easy.

- ✓ = "Good" to "Great"
- ∿ = "Just okay"
- ✗ = "Less than okay" or "Bad"

Grab a pencil, pen or marker and in the top row, make a check mark for the days that were anywhere from "good" to "great." Make a squiggly line for the days that were "just okay." Then mark an X for any days that were "less than okay" or "bad."

In the bottom row, jot down a quick comment explaining why you felt the way you did that day.

Start tonight.

MONDAY	TUESDAY	WEDNESDAY	THURSDAY	FRIDAY	SATURDAY	SUNDAY
Comment	Comment	Comment	Comment	Comment	Comment	Comment

Do a two-minute personal check-in every week. For example, on Sunday evening, write your symbol for the day, and also take a look at your full week. How was it? How did it go? Before you take a long, hard look, think in your head first. Then compare how you feel with how your week actually looks on paper. When you make things visual, physical and tangible (like right above on this piece of paper), they carry much more weight. You can gain insights that may have otherwise been difficult to discover.

Do this for four weeks in a row. Then take a look at the last month of your life in this format and see how it appears. How many check marks, squiggles and Xs do you have? Are you surprised by the result? Or does it generally reflect the way you feel overall?

1. The Act of Bullying

2. Make the connection.

Take a look at your calendar of check marks, squiggles and Xs, and think about these symbols in relation to your outward actions and behaviors over the last month.

What happened on the days when there were check marks?

What happened on the days when there were squiggles?

What happened on the days when there were Xs?

Is there an association you can make? Were good days those when you felt accepted, recognized, appreciated or accomplished? Were bad days associated with negative incidents, or ones that made you feel inadequate, self-doubtful or unseen for who you really are?

Do you notice any patterns? Are there things you can do to maximize your check marks and minimize your Xs, and even squiggles? What are a few ideas you have?

------

3. The people factor.

Sometimes our negative feelings and emotions stem from a person, or several people, in our lives. Maybe they said something rude, or picked a fight with us, or constantly say or do things that make us feel badly. As difficult as it might be, the many ways up all begin with communication.

Talk to them.
Explain how they made you feel.
Tell them why you're approaching them and what ideas you have to fix the issue.

Jot down a few of your ideas.

------

4. Incorporate and integrate.

You see your feelings on paper.
You recognize connections and patterns between your feelings and your behaviors.
You get help and support, and you have thoughts about how to make positive changes.

Now, it's time to take what you've learned and recognized within your life, and incorporate it into your daily routine. The key is baby steps, just one at a time. When we try to blast the rocket ship into outer space without first building and constructing it accordingly, it won't soar like we envisioned.

Look at your marked up calendar each morning. Review the ideas you wrote down about how to make more days check mark days. Try one and evaluate how it works. Have open conversations with people—both the people you have issues with, and the people offering their support to you. Keep it open. Keep it shameless.

1. The Act of Bullying

Write down one positive affirmation (a short statement that makes you feel good, inspired and motivated).

Copy what you wrote above onto a sticky note and put it in a place where you'll see it every day.

> Courage is fire, and bullying is smoke.
> **~ Benjamin Disraeli**

FEEL

If you're bullying others, this behavior isn't coming from nowhere. It is likely that you don't feel your best. Acknowledge those feelings (sad, alone, frustrated, angry, unseen, inadequate).

LEARN

It's important to take the necessary time to learn about yourself and your feelings. The same way we learn a new subject, or watch a how-to YouTube video, sometimes we need to allot some personal time to look within and learn about who we are and what we're going through.

DO

Use your findings and do something with them. Talk to someone. Seek help. Take a step to make it more of a check mark day. Think before you act. Approach people in a new way. Try a different tactic to get what you want.

THE VICTIMIZED

We sat in silence for a few moments. Understanding she needed time but eager to hear her side of the story, I prodded softly, "Can you tell me what happened?"

"Oh, Kaitlyn," she sobbed. "I can't tell you how much I just don't want to talk about it."

"I know it's hard, Rebecca, but I'm here to help you," I insisted.

Her sadness instantly turned to anger, "Help me?" she remarked in disbelief. "Help me?" she repeated, louder this time, "How the hell are you going to help me?"

Confused by her sudden change in disposition, I went on to explain myself, "Well, you can talk it out with me. Maybe I can make you feel better about the situation and hopefully, together, we can come up with a solution to put an end to it."

She laughed sarcastically. "Are you kidding me?"

"What do you mean?" I asked, quite puzzled by her facetious response.

As unprepared as I was for her behavior until now, I was equally shocked for what came next. "Kaitlyn, let me tell you something. You have absolutely no idea what I'm going through. What happened at school yesterday—I don't even want to think about it, not even for a minute. It's been the only thing on my mind ever since. I'm painfully embarrassed and I can't even bear the thought of what other students must think of me…"

"Rebecca, that's—" But she wouldn't let me finish.

"No don't," she said, holding up her hand, "it's horrifying. I don't even know how I made it to school today. I tried so hard to play the sick card with my parents but they knew I wasn't. I just couldn't see her today, you know? Thank goodness I didn't. I don't know what I did to this girl, but she has it in for me."

"How did this happen?" I persisted.

"I didn't do anything, if that's what you're getting at," Rebecca answered defensively.

"I'm not saying that," I assured her.

"Honestly, I was just walking by and unfortunately we made eye contact," I could see the tears begin to stream down her face. "And that was it. She then went off and screamed at me, 'What are you looking at?' I didn't even answer her, I just tried to keep walking but she grabbed my arm and spun me around to face her, put her arm against my neck and slammed me against the lockers, screaming, 'I said, what are you looking at?' I had no idea what to say…" Now Rebecca was crying even harder. "She just kept shoving me deeper and deeper into the lockers as if she was trying to push me right through. She used so much force on my neck that it was actually hard to breathe. No wonder I have a bruise now…"

2. The Victimized

"Oh, Rebecca!" It broke my heart—hearing her account of the incident as I tried, somehow, to understand what she was going through. But I knew I couldn't—and she did too. The hurt, the frustration, the humiliation—it was overwhelming even to think about, let alone experience.

Relieved she told me, but afraid only the wrong words would come out of my mouth, I stayed silent. I wanted to cry too, but I knew it was best to stay strong.

~ Chapter 6, *The Only Way Out*

DISCUSSION QUESTIONS

TAKE A MOMENT
Consider and analyze.

1. Has Rebecca been victimized by the girl she's talking about? If so, how? If not, explain why.

2. In your own words, describe how you believe Rebecca is feeling.

3. Pretend you are Rebecca. What would you have done?

_____

_____

_____

_____

THINGS TO THINK ABOUT

Action is key.

1. When incidents happen such as the one Rebecca is describing in the scene above, there are a whirlwind of feelings, emotions and thoughts that can arise as a result.

2. While it is easy, and even seemingly wise at times, to believe that walking away, leaving it alone, or trying to forget about it, are the best ways forward so as not to create more problems, it is essential that some form of action is seriously considered.

3. The undeniable truth is that if such incidents are left unaddressed, it is possible that even greater problems can arise down the road, both for the victim and others.

WHAT IS A VICTIM?

A victim is defined as someone harmed, injured or killed as a result of an accident, incident, crime, trick or some other form of event.

Let us not focus on labeling someone this way, however, because while they could be "the victim" of an incident in the past, this doesn't mean they always will be. By changing our language slightly, we can effectively reframe the situation. For example, "They were victimized in that scenario."

Why is this important?

Because it denotes the temporary nature of the circumstance. "They *were victimized*" as opposed to "they *are the victim.*"

PEOPLE WHO ARE VICTIMIZED

Unlike people who bully, those who are victimized may encounter such an experience without any prior warning or preparation. They are often blindsided by an incident that makes them out to be a victim on the other side.

If we become victimized, we experience many feelings and emotions, which can include embarrassment, pain, extreme discomfort, inadequacy, shyness, self-doubt, fear and apprehension. No one deserves to be made a victim. While it is awkward, and possibly problematic, to ask, we must pose an insightful question...

WHY WAS I VICTIMIZED?

This is a complex question with a complex answer.

It is absolutely possible that the person doing the bullying, quite simply chose us for no reason whatsoever. Call it being in the wrong place at the wrong time.

The person may have chosen us for reasons we will never fully understand, and that are not valid nor warranted in our eyes.

(Remember: everyone's thoughts and perceptions are different.)

The bullying behavior may have been directed towards us because the person perceived us as being weak or more vulnerable, or of having less power than them.

(Remember: people who bully do it to feel power or control over another.)

The person may have been egged on, pressured or encouraged by others to bully.

(Remember: peer pressure is one of the reasons people bully others, because the person doing the bullying wants to feel accepted—stemming from insecurities.)

If indeed there was a reason behind why *we* were selected to be bullied, how would that make us feel? What if we had control over whether or not that reason existed, and we could make easy changes in our lives to combat and even eliminate it?

Being the victim of an unfavorable situation is not easy. Depending on the nature of the encounter and how you handle it, there may be post-traumatic scars you're left with. This is no small matter. The power lies in our choices from this point forward. We can always *choose* how we act and react. We can learn and train ourselves to speak and behave in ways that empower and liberate us.

MOVING FORWARD

Think of animals in the wild. Most of them face the risk of being eaten. The threat of predation puts a tremendous amount of selective pressure on animals, which affects their ability to survive in specific environments and prompts them to adopt numerous behavioral strategies that increase their chances. This is a two-part process:

1. Identify a predatory threat
2. Use effective strategies to avoid being detected and attacked

2. The Victimized

For animals, recognizing the cues of a predator nearby is absolutely essential so that they may begin their anti-predator behavior. Failure to execute this first step will likely result in failure to carry out the second step, which can then lead to a fatal outcome.

Humans can be much the same.

Before we go on the reactive or defensive, we must first detect the potential for predatory behavior. If we feel threatened, that's when we are more likely to kick our protective behaviors into high gear. It's fight or flight.

If an animal fails at its attempt to remain undetected by its predator, then it must move on to the next plan: use strategies to improve its chances of surviving the encounter. When the animal prey lives with a large group, it can signal the group and scare the predator away before an attack takes place. If the animal prey is physically fit, it can signal to predators that any form of an attack would be a waste of time. (Did you know some lizard species do push-ups to show their strength in order to fend off potential competitors and predators?)

If we think of potentially harmful scenarios similar to animals, there are opportunities for us to show that: *We are not to be bullied. We are not to be messed with. We are not to be the target of negative and defeating behaviors.*

Here are a few ways to do that:

- We sense danger, notify our friends and band together so there are too many of us against just one bully.
- We show our personal strength (mental, emotional and physical), sending a clear message to those around us.
- We use our voice (open communication, speaking up) to demonstrate the fact that silence is not an option for us.

The same way a dog can sense fear, so too can human beings sense the same in another person. We use cues, subconscious and conscious, to detect fear in other people. We can identify a few of the most obvious physical signs of fear within ourselves: increased heartrate, stomach butterflies or digestive changes, trembling muscles, sweating and chills. Identifying fear in others might look like little to no eye contact, caving and hunched shoulders, fidgeting, attempted avoidance and running away.

A study conducted by Utrecht University in the Netherlands suggests that humans communicate via smell, just like other animals. The findings of the study were published on November 5, 2012 in the journal, *Psychological Science*, and state that humans can actually smell fear and disgust. Couple this with our ability to read social and humanistic cues, and it seems rather straightforward for us to sense fear in others.

While we cannot control the way anyone else acts, we *can* control our own actions and behaviors. One element of bullying behavior widely agreed upon by experts is *control*. Bullies want to know they have control over someone else's emotions. This means it is incredibly important to show your *impermeability*, both before and after an encounter.

In this sense, to be impermeable is to be *unaffected*. No matter what someone says or does, you remain untouched. They cannot "get you."

So, how can we minimize our chances of being victimized and demonstrate to everyone around us that we are *impermeable*?

Let us start from within and move outwards.

ACTIONABLE TASKS

1. Focus on your self-esteem.

The following exercises you can do anytime. They can also be repeated periodically. Building and maintaining your self-esteem is something you can focus on throughout your entire life. When you have high self-esteem, it's easy to feel happy and fulfilled across a wide range of scenarios in your life—even difficult ones.

2. The Victimized

A. How would you describe yourself? (Think of your personality and character.)

Read what you wrote. Do you like how it sounds? Does it have a positive or negative connotation (or both)?

B. In the box below, write down a list of three things you like about yourself.

THINGS I LIKE ABOUT MYSELF
1.
2.
3.

Read what you wrote. Do you like what you see? Was it easy or difficult to think of three things to jot down?

Can you think of more than three? Go ahead and write those down, too.

Didn't make it to three? Write down things you *want to* or *could* like about yourself.

C. Most of us have at least a couple things we don't like about ourselves. Write down three things that come to mind in the box below.

THINGS I DON'T LIKE ABOUT MYSELF
1.
2.
3.

Read what you wrote. How do you feel about what you see in this list? Was it easy or difficult to think of three things?

Are there more than three in your mind? Go ahead and write those down, too.

Didn't make it to three? That's a good thing!

Now, here comes an important question:

Are the things in this list changeable or unchangeable about yourself?

For example, let's say one of the items in your second column is "height." Well, this is something you simply cannot change. You could wear high heels or thicker soles in your shoes, perhaps, but that's only a little temporary fun. It's time to come to terms with how tall or short you are because there is absolutely nothing you can do about it. Instead of this last statement being frustrating or maddening, let it come as a form of relief. No control? Accept and move on.

If one of the things on your list is your temper, your mood, your muscle mass, your job or your grades in school, all of these are within your control.

If you're not happy with how bad your temper is, and you feel as though you're always walking a fine line between keeping your cool and completely losing it, talk to someone, seek the help of a professional and work on it to make a positive change. In a bad mood all the time? Focus your efforts on figuring out why and make moves to address the root of your unhappiness.

Wish you had greater muscle mass? Ask a parent to give you some strengthening exercises in your home gym. Or do a few sessions with a personal trainer who can educate you, and show you safe and effective ways to build muscle.

Bad part-time job? Give your letter of resignation and find a new one. Poor grades in school? Study harder, ask your teacher for extra help, get a tutor, don't miss classes and do the work to pull them up.

> God, grant me the serenity to accept the things I cannot change, the courage to change the things I can, and the wisdom to know the difference.
> **~ Benjamin Disraeli**

If you are able to be honest with yourself in these lists, you're already well on your way to building your self-esteem. It can be a lifelong process, too. Personal development has no beginning and no end, and sometimes we all need reminders of how great we really are, whether there are things we'd like to change about ourselves or not.

2. Eye contact.

Eye contact is a powerful thing, yet easy to learn and do (or not do). It is something to be mindful of as you go about your daily life. Do you look at people's eyes? During conversation? While walking by? Do you naturally avoid making eye contact because you find it uncomfortable?

When delivered at the right time and in the right way, making eye contact, or *not* making eye contact, can demonstrate your impermeability.

A. To a potential aggressor, intentional, confident and strong eye contact can demonstrate that you will not be intimidated, nor easily be made into a victim.

If you believe someone is considering some form of negative action towards you, use your eyes. No matter what the glare, stare or seemingly negative look they throw your way, be sure your eyes make contact with theirs. Then, do not break this eye contact. Hold your expression. There's no need to respond with any kind of "look" in return, just focus on your eyes. Imagine they are daggers of self-confidence and self-defense, and it's up to you to prove that these daggers should *not* be crossed. This may seem overly simple right now and you might be wondering how a little thing like maintaining eye contact can send a message of strength to another person. This strategy, however, has the ability to exude a level of self-assuredness that says, "I know who I am. I love who I am. I'm aware of my individual rights and I deserve the best. You can't mess with me, so don't even try it."

B. Avoidance of eye contact with a suspicious or dangerous person can be the best form of self-defense because it avoids misinterpretations and does not initiate communication with a potentially aggressive person.

Think of a time when you were fully aware of someone looking at you, even though you weren't looking at them. We can often sense this. Particularly if a threatening person is trying to get our attention or make a scene, the best defense is often no eye contact at all. Look straight ahead. Be sure the gaze of your eyes is level (not low to the ground or way up high in the sky). Carry on walking or doing whatever it is that you're doing, and play it off as though you are completely oblivious to them. Usually this results in the other person giving up, and you avoiding a negative situation.

3. Body language.

Let's consider the way in which we carry ourselves. Picture the way we walk into a room. How is our posture? Are our shoulders hunched or do we press them back? Is the general gaze of our eyes high or low? Do we look down a lot, or up and around? The next best thing after making eye contact and maintaining it is moving through the world around us with a strong and sure physical demeanor. It looks like this:

- Shoulders down (not shrugged up)
- Shoulder blades pressed together (chest slightly out)
- Eyes gazing outwards and straight ahead (not down nor up)
- Arms hanging naturally, swinging freely as we walk, or holding something (no fidgeting or clenching)

4. Talk.

Write down your answers to the following questions.

A. Have you ever been bullied or made to be the victim somehow?

B. If yes, how? Describe what happened.

C. How did you respond or react in the moment, and afterwards?

D. Did the situation escalate?

....

....

E. Would you do anything differently next time? What would your advice be for someone else?

....

....

If you find yourself in a situation where you are being victimized, the most important action you can take is to TALK.

Talk to your perpetrator. Speak up. Stand up for yourself. If you do it right away, with strength and self-assuredness, you immediately show that you are not a victim. Remember, bullies want to know they have control over someone else's emotions. So, show them that they *don't*.

Talk to your parents, friends, teachers, guidance counselors, relatives—whoever you feel most comfortable with and you know will listen. Say what's going on, get the help and support you need. You are far from alone, so there's no need to act like you are.

Talk through email or text. Is speaking up face-to-face too intimidating right now? Can't yet make a phone call? That's okay. Start smaller and easier. Try sending a text, email or instant message to someone you trust.

Talk to yourself. Remind yourself that you're better than this. You deserve more—*much* more. And you won't stand for this kind of treatment. We're all equals. We're all but mere human beings, experiencing life on this earth together. And when we see this big-picture view for what it is, the rest becomes crystal clear. No person has the right to treat another badly. Speak to yourself the same way you would speak to your favorite person. Treat yourself with respect and

2. The Victimized

be the champion of your own thoughts. You can be your own worst enemy or your own best friend. The choice is yours.

Start somewhere, anywhere. Yes, instructing someone to "talk openly and speak up" is much easier said than done for many of us. Instead of focusing on how difficult or scary it is, take one small step. Can't say anything to your perpetrator just yet? Tell a friend. Not ready to say it out loud? Write it down. Talk about it to yourself behind closed doors. Just start. Somewhere. Anywhere. Use your words.

> Speak your mind even if your voice shakes.
> ~ **Maggie Kuhn**

FEEL

Allow yourself to experience the emotions associated with being victimized. Cast shame and embarrassment aside. Before you can move on, you must give yourself the grace to truly FEEL.

LEARN

Know that it is not your fault. You do not deserve to be made a victim, and you have a right to fair and equal treatment. There are things you can do ensure that you are not victimized again.

DO

Move. Act. Step in the right direction. Talk. Turn inwards. Take the time to focus on YOU. Adopt simple yet effective strategies in your everyday life that enable you to feel great about yourself and be impermeable to acts of bullying towards you.

3

THE BYSTANDER

My face grew hot and my palms began to sweat as I realized how little control we had over the situation.

Marcel leaned in and put his arm around me. As much as it felt good to be comforted, I couldn't help but think that the real person in need of comfort was Rebecca and yet she was the very person pushing away all those in her life capable of providing it.

Who did I think I was? What could I really do to help the situation? I planned to follow up with the guidance counselor Marcel had spoken to, but then what? I knew very well that whatever punishment the school gave Chantel—if any at all—likely wouldn't faze her. How could I take matters into my own hands? Chantel was intimidating. The very look in her eyes told you she was fearless, aggressive and capable of hateful acts others wouldn't dream of. What if I were to stand up to her? What would it take to get through to her? It seemed to me that the only way to have an impact on someone like Chantel was to communicate with her in a way she understood—on her level. Threats, physical violence, verbal abuse—this was the kind of approach to which Chantel might—just might—have a reaction. But how could I stoop to such a level? How I could I at once forget about my pride, my dignity and my demeanor. The likelihood of me, little old me, having even the slightest positive effect on the situation was slim to none. But there was a deeper truth at play here. A shameful fact. Plain and simple, I was afraid—afraid to be a target. I feared deeply that if I stood up to Chantel, her focus might make a fateful switch. I might become…her next victim.

~ Chapter 5, *The Only Way Out*

Although I was grateful for the fact that Rebecca had opened up to me at least a little, it wasn't enough. I was profoundly worried about her and I feared that over time, matters would only worsen. Our conversation was so brief that I didn't even have a chance to ask her if there had been other incidents between her and Chantel. Even without an answer, my instincts told me there were—and if I was right, this would only further prove my prediction that another encounter was just around the corner.

And yet here I lay, still in my bed—a silenced friend. From my perspective, I wasn't a friend at all…far from it, in fact. A real friend would have told someone, spoken out, taken action in some way. But I didn't. As much as I felt the opposing, contradictory pulls of my dilemma

3. The Bystander

deep inside, I was far too afraid to disobey Rebecca's wishes. She'd confided in me that night. Even though it was only for a few minutes and despite the fact that it ended badly, there was still meaning in it. Didn't Rebecca need a friend more than anything else right now? If I turned against her, all trust would be lost. She'd dismiss me the same way she had earlier that morning.

As my mind's whirlwind of thoughts began to spiral in the opposite direction, I felt my eyes grow heavy and tired. I blinked once and then slowly reopened my eyes to the darkness around me. No, I told myself, keeping quiet was the best way. How could I betray my best friend? How could I even contemplate going against her wishes after everything she'd been through? And who knows, perhaps Rebecca was right. These kinds of incidents happen all the time. Kids get over it and bullies grow up. I wasn't the one on the other end of the attacks. How could I possibly understand what she was going through and how she felt? Who was I to decide what was best? I'd believed in Rebecca all my life. Why was I second-guessing her judgment now? Just as she said, it was her life and her business. It was my duty to respect her wishes.

~ Chapter 7, *The Only Way Out*

In both of the quoted sections above from the novel, *The Only Way Out*, we are invited to hear the inner dialogue of a bystander. Notice the opposing sides and contradictory thoughts.

DISCUSSION QUESTIONS

TAKE A MOMENT
Consider it.

1. What makes this person a bystander?

2. What feelings and emotions does the bystander have? What other feelings, emotions and thoughts do you think bystanders experience in these types of situations?

3. What do you believe a bystander ought to do (or not do) in a situation like this?

THINGS TO THINK ABOUT

Action is key.

1. Being a bystander isn't easy and it brings with it a myriad of contemplations and considerations, especially when the victimized person is a friend.

2. While there are many factors and elements that a bystander considers as they deliberate on how to handle the information they know, *action* (of one kind or another) is essential.

3. Remaining a bystander is an entirely useless role, because if we are bystanders, we have critical information that we decline to share or do anything with. It is an abject waste. If, on the other hand, we can find the courage to stand up for the people in our community, to act as part of a collective group and to be *up*standers, then we have a chance to ignite change and make a difference.

3. The Bystander

WHAT IS A BYSTANDER?

The definition of a bystander by way of the dictionary is "a person who is present at an event or incident but does not take part." We're going to take this one step further and state that a bystander is also "someone who knows or is aware of a particular event or incident and does not participate, nor speak up."

There are far fewer people who may have witnessed or seen an incident of bullying, compared to the number of people who come to know about it. Both forms of bystanders have their respective roles to play in the bigger picture. Especially in consideration of the heightened occurrences and elevated rates of cyberbullying, the latter half of the bystander definition must be incorporated into the conversation. Bullying is not what it used to be. Now, those who do the bullying no longer have to stand up to someone face-to-face, they can simply type or speak through a smartphone or computer. In these cases, there are no (or very few) actual witnesses of the bullying taking place, but once it is up online, it may reach hundreds, thousands, even millions of others. Are they not bystanders, too?

PEOPLE WHO ARE BYSTANDERS

In line with the more traditional definition, there are four types of bystanders:

1. **Assistants**—help the person or people doing the bullying and join in
2. **Reinforcers**—give support to the person or people doing the bullying
3. **Outsiders**—stay away, do not take sides and do not give any kind of silent approval
4. **Defenders**—comfort the person being bullied, and actively try to stop the bullying

I'm going to add a fifth type here, called the **Knowers**. The knowers are the kinds of bystanders who are aware of bullying incidents that have taken place and who either choose to speak up and defend, or remain silent like the Outsiders.

People who find themselves bystanders are faced with many challenging emotions and inner struggles, typically centered around the critical question:

What should I do with the information I have?

When close friendships are at stake and when there is a fear of becoming victimized ourselves, the next move can become clouded, unclear and scary. Deep down we may know that action is needed, and yet, complicated emotions and fears cause us to hesitate and think twice. We do not want to do further harm to our friend or ourselves, and yet we do not want the bullying behavior to continue.

IMAGINE

Comparing scenarios.

Close your eyes and imagine for a moment. You are walking down the hall on your way to class and you see a student push another student into the lockers, knock their books down, and then call them "loser" as they walk away laughing.

What is your first instinct of what to do next?

SCENARIO 1: YOU SPEAK UP AND ACTIVELY GET HELP

Suppose your instinct is to take outward action. Maybe you report the incident, confront the bullied individual or talk to the person doing the bullying. You attempt to stop any further incidents from taking place.

What is the ideal outcome in your mind?

------

3. The Bystander

Think of the possibilities for yourself, the bullied person, the bully and the community.

SCENARIO 2: YOU KEEP IT TO YOURSELF AND LET IT GO

In this case, your instincts drive you to stay silent. You keep the information to yourself and you carry on.

What is the ideal outcome in your mind?

Think of the possibilities for yourself, the bullied person, the bully and the community.

WRONG PLACE, WRONG TIME

Sometimes life has a way of putting us in the wrong place at the wrong time. Or, perhaps it's the right place at the right time because we are "meant to be there", even though we don't know how or why just yet.

Since we are not the active bully, we have no control over the situation—at first, that is. We find ourselves witness to something, and then we come to ask ourselves, *what do I do?* We didn't choose to be there. We didn't decide to see what we saw or become aware of an unwelcome incident. But after it happens, there's nothing we can do about changing what has already taken place. There may be part of us that wants to pretend it never happened and to live on wishing it will all go away. This, of course, will never work. We must then accept that we cannot control what has already happened and focus on what we *can* control: the actions we take next.

HAVE A RESPONSIBILITY

Whether we can immediately accept it or not, we have a responsibility. We've seen something. Or we know something. It's possible that others who may have seen or become aware of what happened do not have the will or the courage to do anything about it. Understand this one fact: if we do nothing, nothing will change. And yet change is absolutely possible for one person, one situation, or many people and many situations—just as long as that first step takes place.

MOVING FORWARD

First and foremost, stay safe.

Use everything you have at your disposal to make an intelligent and informed decision that puts your own personal safety and the safety of others in top priority. Don't do anything that you believe may be dangerous, and be sure to involve someone in a position in authority if necessary.

SILENCE OR ACTION?

If you choose silence and denial, there is no moving forward. Silence keeps us still and stagnant. It might even propel the situation backwards in the sense that when troubling things are not dealt with and are left to fester, they can eat away at us mentally and physically, and can even lead to the situation repeating itself since the negative behaviors were not addressed or met with any form of consequence the first time.

To get somewhere we haven't been before, we must move—we must take action, no matter how big or small.

Maybe you tell your parents what you know.
Maybe you talk to the bullied person to make a plan together.
Maybe you report the incident to a higher authority, such as your teacher or the school principal.
Maybe you use the strength of your community to build power in numbers, banding in groups to protect one another.

Your movement might look like one of these actions, or many of them, or something else entirely. What it is matters less than the action itself. Bottom line, it is *something*.

ACTIONABLE TASKS

Think about a bullying incident you've seen or that you are aware of. If nothing comes to mind, imagine you see a student getting their basketball taken away by a group of older students who push, shove and tease them almost every day at recess. Or, imagine you find cruel posts and comments on social media about one of your classmates.

1. Acceptance.

Accept the fact that you've seen or know something that you wish you didn't. This part you cannot change. Ask yourself the following questions and write your answers in the blank spaces below.

A. What did you see or what do you know?

_____

_____

B. How bad is it? Rate it on a scale of 1 (minor) to 10 (major).

_____

_____

C. What is likely to happen if you do nothing? What are some possible outcomes?

_____

_____

D. What is likely to happen if you do something?

_____

_____

2. Working through it.

What's done is done. Now, it's time to focus on the impact this has had on you. Ask yourself the following questions and write your answers in the blank spaces below.

A. How did you feel the moment you saw the incident or heard about it?

_____

_____

B. Does anything about it make you uneasy or fearful?

C. List a few ideas you have of how you might be able to reduce your uneasiness and fear around the situation.

D. Which ideas from #3 above do you believe are most reasonable and realistic? Are there one or more that you can begin to execute as early as today?

3. Developing a plan.

You've accepted what has already happened. You've acknowledged your feelings. Now it's time to figure out what to do next.

A. Write down the name of the first person who comes to mind who you feel most comfortable talking to about this.

B. Write down what you want to say.

C. If there is a second or third step that you believe ought to come after you talk to the person you confide in, write those down.

_____

_____

D. What are the possibilities from here? (Feel free to think of both the positive and negative sides.)

_____

_____

_____

E. How do you think you will feel after you've talked and spoken up?

_____

_____

_____

> Strong people stand up for themselves. But the strongest people stand up for others.

FEEL

Show yourself grace. It's okay to feel all kinds of conflicting emotions. Give yourself the time you need to process the situation. Avoid denial.

LEARN

The role of the bystander can be deeply impactful. Because you have witnessed an incident or you know of an incident, you are put in a position with the potential to act on it. And it may just be the case that the victim cannot stand up for themselves, leaving you with an opportunity to make a difference.

DO

Figure out how you can make a move. Talk—to the victim, to the bully, to the school, to your parents, to your friends—and start exploring the many ways in which you may be able to break the cycle by opening the dialogue, thereby minimizing the chance of additional incidents taking place.

4

SOCIAL MEDIA AND CYBERBULLYING

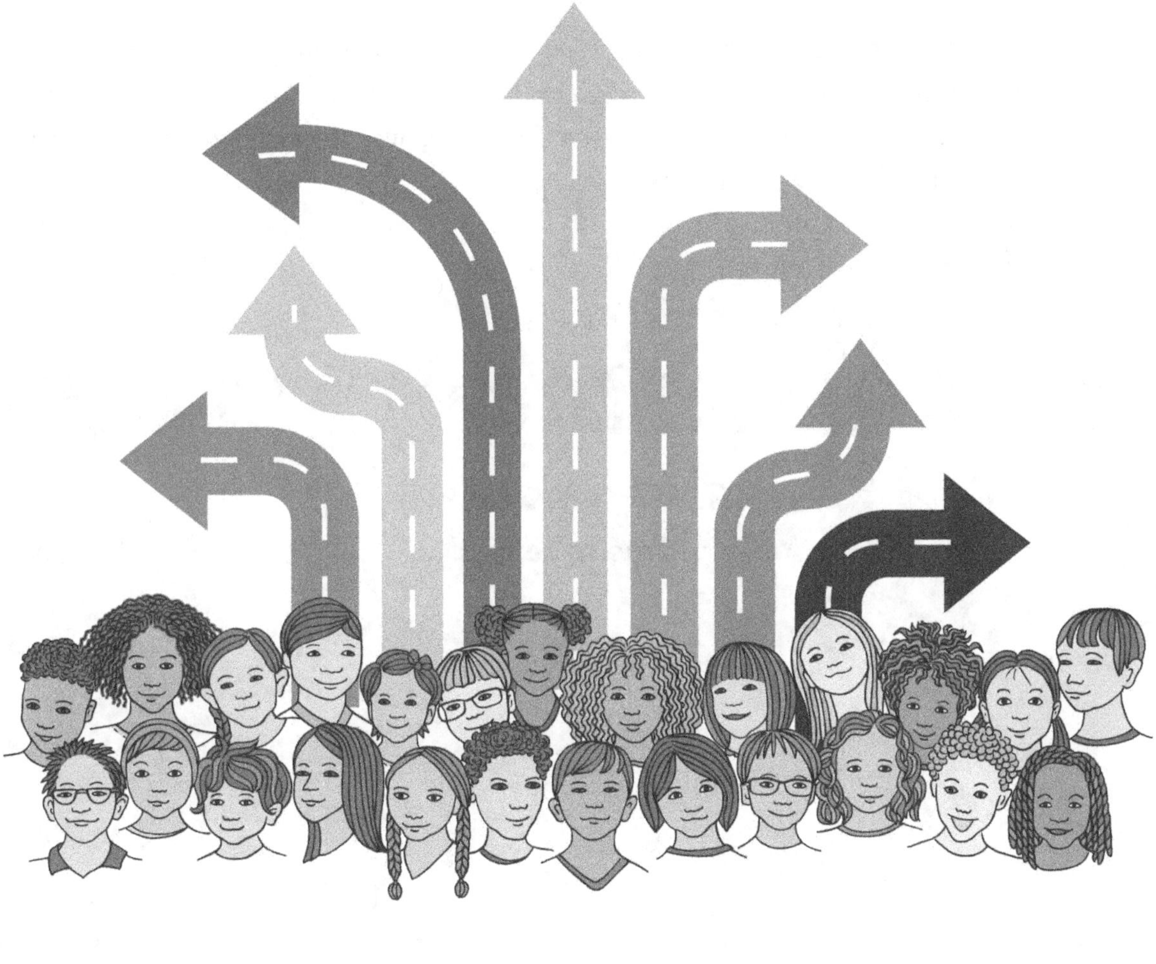

"*Rebecca wasn't only bullied at school. It was happening online too.*"
My heart began to pound through my rib cage. I held my hand to my chest and muttered, "Nooo..."

"I know it must be hard to hear," the girl kept talking. Half of me wanted her to continue but the other half dreaded each new word she spoke.

....

"And what was posted on her Facebook feed was awful...just so, so awful."
"What? What was it? What did people post there? And who posted? Was it Chantel? Or other people too?" I spewed out the questions fast, unable to contain myself.
The girl seemed a little startled. "It was all Chantel. But there were other kids liking her comments."
I pulled the tablet a little closer and began reading. The comments started out in a taunting manner and progressively worsened as the days went on. The first few were strictly from Chantel, but as the girl explained, even though she was the instigator, many others participated in the evil act on a more secondary level.

~ **Chapter 21,** *The Only Way Out*

DISCUSSION QUESTIONS

TAKE A MOMENT
Time to reflect.

1. How do you think this cyberbullying affected Rebecca?

---

4. Social Media and Cyberbullying

2. Have you ever come across evidence of cyberbullying? Describe what you saw.

   _____

   _____

   _____

3. What would you do if you were cyberbullied?

   _____

   _____

   _____

THINGS TO THINK ABOUT

Understanding the good and the bad.

1. Technological innovation has made our world and our individual lives highly digitized. This has become even further exacerbated by the COVID-19 pandemic.

2. On one hand, digital technologies make our lives easier by facilitating business, aiding in communication, helping governments and giving us unlimited access to information. On the other hand, these technologies also complicate our lives and have negative consequences, one of which is cyberbullying.

3. By heightening our awareness and deepening our understanding, we can better manage and handle digital technologies, including social media.

WHAT IS CYBERBULLYING?

Cyberbullying, also known as online bullying, is a type of bullying or harassment that uses electronic tools and digital devices, including cell phones, tablets and computers. It has become more common over the last several years, especially among youth and adolescents, with advancements in technology and the growing digital space. It can happen through text, SMS and smartphone apps, as well as online in social media, gaming and forums.

Cyberbullying is when someone posts, sends or shares negative content about someone else. This content can be false, harmful or mean, and can even be personal or private information about the other person, which can make them feel embarrassed or humiliated.

The most common places where cyberbullying can take place are:

- Social media (TikTok, Snapchat, YouTube, Instagram, Facebook)
- Text message and instant messaging apps
- Direct messaging and online chatting on the Internet
- Online chat rooms, message boards and forums
- Online gaming communities
- Email

Just like in-person bullying, cyberbullying statistics are alarming, too.

1 in 3 children suffers from bullying worldwide
(Source: StopBullying.org, UNESCO)

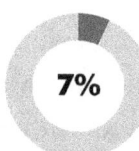
7% of Canadians experience cyberbullying
(Source: 150 Stat Can)

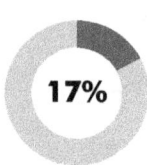
17% of Canadian young adults aged 18–24 suffer from cyberbullying
(Source: 150 Stat Can)

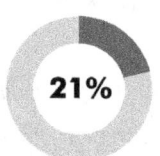
21% of Americans between the ages of 10 and 18 have been cyberbullied
(Source: Security.org)

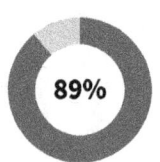
89% of teachers believe that cyberbullying in Canada is the leading safety issue in public schools
(Source: Canadian Red Cross)

4. Social Media and Cyberbullying

IMPACT ON MENTAL HEALTH AND WELLBEING

Let's take a look at the prevalence of cyberbullying on social networks.

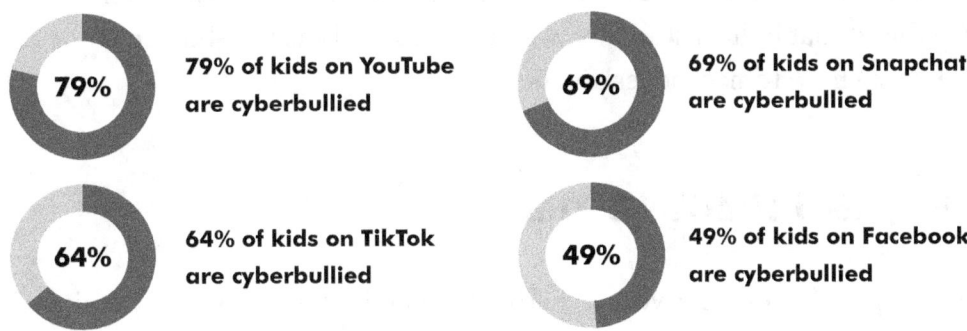

79% — 79% of kids on YouTube are cyberbullied

69% — 69% of kids on Snapchat are cyberbullied

64% — 64% of kids on TikTok are cyberbullied

49% — 49% of kids on Facebook are cyberbullied

(Source: Security.org)

Cyberbullying can have very serious negative effects on children, youth and young adults. More specifically, it can impact a person's mental health and wellbeing in a number of ways. What makes cyberbullying so concerning is the fact that its negative impacts can be both short and long term, and tend to extend far beyond the repercussions of physical bullying, in the sense that it attacks more profound areas of our mind.

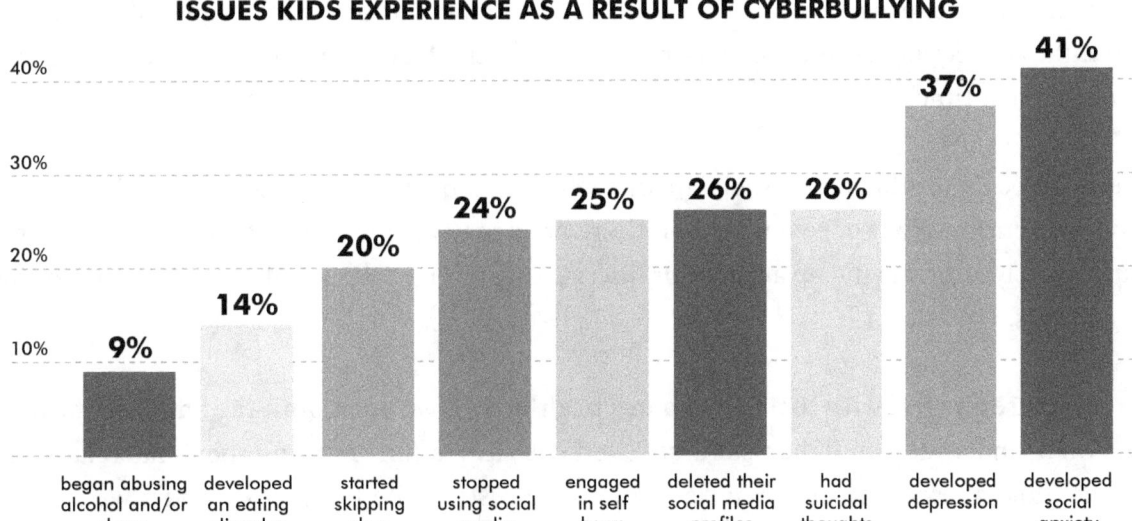

ISSUES KIDS EXPERIENCE AS A RESULT OF CYBERBULLYING

- began abusing alcohol and/or drugs: 9%
- developed an eating disorder: 14%
- started skipping class: 20%
- stopped using social media: 24%
- engaged in self harm: 25%
- deleted their social media profiles: 26%
- had suicidal thoughts: 26%
- developed depression: 37%
- developed social anxiety: 41%

Effects of Cyberbullying
(Source: Ditch the Label Study)

47

According to the Cyberbullying Research Center, 64% of people who have been cyberbullied say it negatively affects their ability to feel safe and learn at school. The Center for Disease Control conducted a study which found that students who have been cyberbullied have trouble adjusting to school and are more likely to have behavioral and mental health issues. Gini and Pozzoli's research study found that bullied students were twice as likely as non-bullied students to have physical ailments such as stomachaches and headaches.

MANAGING AND LIMITING TIME

Research shows a possible link between cyberbullying and long hours spent online. The University of Georgia conducted a study which found that higher social media addiction scores and more hours spent online predicted cyberbullying behavior.

We must acknowledge the fact that youth and young adults are still in the process of developing mentally and intellectually. Social media and other digital technologies give them a worldwide audience, and we are simply expecting them to make good decisions on their own. Young people online are adapting to different social norms from those in person. It is extremely common for people to be more critical and aggressive on the internet because they are anonymous and can easily avoid retaliation. Cyberbullies also feel less remorse and empathy than physical bullies because they don't see the impact that their actions have on the people they bully. There are no natural consequences and no opportunities to learn from their mistakes so they can act differently next time.

It is easy to become addicted to social media, which means that we crave it when we are not on it, and we continue to use it even though there are negative consequences such as feeling tired during the day after staying up at night online, getting poor grades in school, or having conflicts with parents.

In order to use and live with social media in a healthy way, we must limit the amount of time we spend on it, and understand the risks associated with it. We can define our personal relationship with technology, examine our own self-worth and restrict the number of hours we spend on social media platforms.

4. Social Media and Cyberbullying

Here are a few tips to reduce social media usage:

1. Keep social media apps out of sight so they're not on your mind (remove notifications).
2. Pre-set parameters and time limits on your social media apps.
3. Don't bring your phone to the dinner table.
4. Leave your phone outside your bedroom.
5. Commit to doing a phone-free activity for 30 minutes every day.

MOVING FORWARD

Whether you are not yet involved in social media and other online digital outlets, or you are already active on a regular basis, it is important to make yourself aware of a few things.

1. The content you post and share online through your accounts can be viewed by friends and family, but also acquaintances and strangers.
2. Everything you post and share is always there, and it creates a permanent record of your activities, behaviors, likes, dislikes and opinions. Think of this like your online reputation.
3. Anyone and everyone can look you up online and see your profile, including schools, clubs, employers and others.
4. Cyberbullying can harm online reputations, not only of the person doing the bullying, but also of those participating and getting bullied.

At school and in the community, we must acknowledge the unique aspects of cyberbullying that make it particularly concerning:

- **Difficult to pinpoint**
  Because cyberbullying happens through people's personal digital devices, teachers, parents and fellow friends might not hear or see it. This makes it harder to recognize and offer help.

- **Persistent**
  People have their digital devices on them all the time. This makes it possible to communicate quickly and continuously 24 hours a day. Therefore, if someone is experiencing cyberbullying, it's hard for them to find any relief.

- **Permanent**
  If it isn't reported and removed, most content that we communicate digitally is public and permanent. If we're involved in cyberbullying, this can have negative impacts on our lives down the road if we try to get a job, get into university or join a club.

ACTIONABLE TASKS

1. Make a diagram.

Fill in the blanks with two things that contribute to cyberbullying. Consider factors that make cyberbullying behavior more likely, especially when they exist together and at the same time.

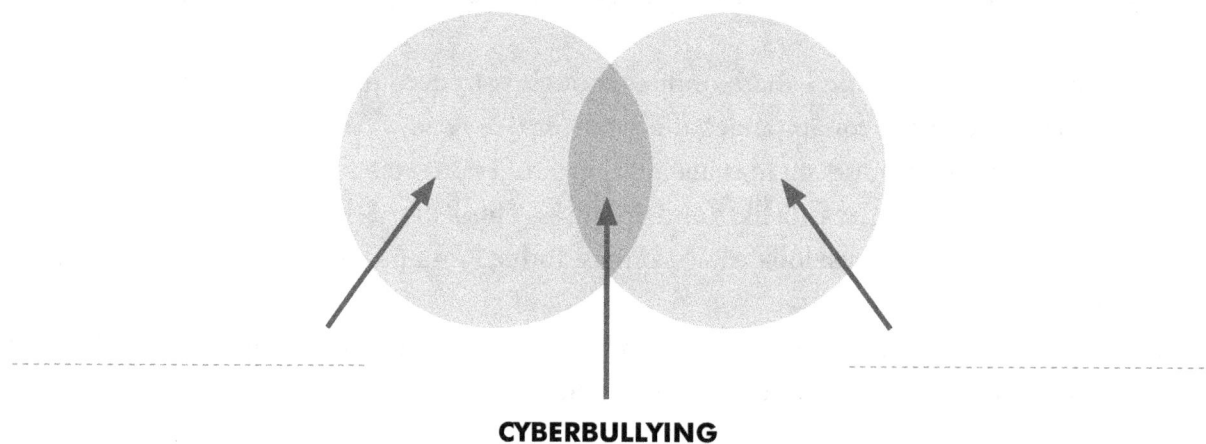

CYBERBULLYING

2. Make a list.

Write down three things you enjoy doing that do not involve the use of a digital device (including television).

1. _____
2. _____
3. _____

3. Spot the signs.

Young people are using the internet more now than ever before. Unfortunately, cyberbullying happens right in the comfort of our own homes. Even when someone is being cyberbullied, they don't always realize the severity of it. They might not know they need help or that help is available, or it's possible they feel too embarrassed to talk about it. Knowing what to look for so you can spot the signs early is important, and can potentially save a person hours of torment, unhappiness and mental struggle.

According to the National Crime Prevention Council, there are three main areas to be aware of:

- **Emotional**
    → Becomes more shy or withdrawn
    → Becomes anxious or stressed
    → Appears moody and agitated
    → Shows signs of depression
    → Shows signs of aggressive behavior

- **Academic**
    → Stops wanting to go to school and loses interest
    → Skips school
    → Gets in trouble at school
    → Grades drop

- **Social and Behavioral**
    → *Stops using their digital device or computer* (biggest red flag!)
    → Changes friends
    → Doesn't want to participate in activities they used to enjoy
    → Changes their eating or sleeping habits, or starts having nightmares
    → Hurts themselves, or attempts or threatens suicide

There are also signs we can look out for to identify when a young person might be cyberbullying others:

- Appears jumpy or nervous when they're using their cell phone or computer
- Seems secretive about what they're doing on their digital device
- Spends a lot of their time on digital devices
- Stops using their digital device the moment anyone comes near
- Becomes very angry or upset if cell phone or computer use is limited or taken away

4. Know what to do if cyberbullying takes place.

If you're being cyberbullied, it is critical that you act on it right away so that you reduce the likelihood of it continuing and becoming repetitive and persistent. If you know someone who is being cyberbullied, talk to them, lend a helping hand if you feel able, and educate them about how to prevent and handle it.

- **Block the bully.**
  According to young people and the National Crime Prevention Council, <u>the most effective way to stop and prevent cyberbullying is to block the bully</u>.

- **Ask the bully to stop.**
  Send a private message or post publicly online, and directly ask the cyberbully to stop their behavior towards you (or your friend).

- **Talk to someone about what is going on.**
  Pick a person you trust and tell them about the cyberbullying you're experiencing. Preferably, choose someone in a position of authority (parents, teacher, counselor) so that the behavior can be proactively and sternly addressed, stopped and prevented from continuing.

- **Engage a professional.**
  Get an expert to help you set up appropriate safeguards and blocking measures on your devices.

4. Social Media and Cyberbullying

- **Identify it.**
Especially online, it can be difficult to determine whether someone is just having fun or deliberately trying to hurt you. Bottom line, if you feel hurt or think people are laughing *at* you instead of with you, the joke has gone too far.

- **Use the tools.**
Every social platform has different tools that let you restrict who can view your profile, comment and connect with you. There are also ways to report cases of cyberbullying. Use them.

- **Words matter.**
Whether it's for you or a friend, your words can make a difference. Talk about what you're going through or comfort your friend to let them know you're there for them. Cyberbullying can be life-threatening so it's crucial that you talk openly. Bullies need to be called out and made aware that their behavior is not acceptable nor will it be tolerated.

> A keyboard away doesn't make it okay.

FEEL

If you feel hurt by someone's online behavior towards you, it isn't right and you don't have to stand for it.

LEARN

Once you've identified cyberbullying, acknowledge the fact that it is serious and can have very significant negative repercussions. It's no joke, and your action to stop it is critical.

DO

Report it. Talk to someone you trust. Stick up for a friend. Block the cyberbully and tell them to stop their behavior towards you or someone else. Limit your time spent online. Know the tools available to you. Be safe and proactive in all your digital social actions.

5

FRIENDSHIP

> *The dearest of friends we were—sharing similar interests, enjoying highly entertaining play dates and always spending as much time together as possible. During our elementary years, Rebecca attended a French immersion school in our local town and I a public school. And now finally the time had come. We'd be together.*
>
> ~ **Chapter 2**, *The Only Way Out*

THE VALUE OF FRIENDSHIPS

Friendship is a beautiful thing. Fundamentally different from solid family relationships, friendships give us social connection, a sense of belonging and a certain validation of who we are. With the right friends, we can feel happy, settled and content as we make our way through life. Studies have proven that the sense of belonging and togetherness we get from friendships can promote mental health, physical wellbeing and an improved focus on learning.

In another sense, particularly as we grow as individuals, while we can place great weight on family acceptance and love, it can be even more validating and satisfying to feel that from our friends. "Oh, that's just Mom and Dad" versus "Wow, the connection I have with this friend is truly rewarding."

Let's face it: in our adolescent years, most of us go through a period of time when we would much rather spend time away from our families than with them. Instead of thinking of this phenomenon negatively, I invite you to see it for what it is. Scientists and psychologists will tell you that teens pull away from their parents due to a biological instinct to separate themselves in preparation for adulthood. Taking it a step further, when a teen pushes one or both parents away, believe it or not, it is often because of their strong sense of security in the relationship. They take it for granted, but usually this is only temporary. When we are adolescents, the emotional distance we put between ourselves and our families is our way of exploring our independence and learning to deal with the personal issues we experience along the way.

Given that this is so, it comes as no great surprise that we take our friendships very seriously. As we should. Friends love one another, friends spend time together, friends share secrets, friends protect and stick up for each other. The relationship is trusted and sacred. We must treasure it, nurture it, work for it and maintain it.

THE BEAUTIES AND THE COMPLEXITIES

Friendships can be beautiful. They can also be equally complex. A friendship can make us feel fulfilled in a variety of ways. That same friendship can also make us feel empty and lost. Sometimes the admiration and caring nature between two friends can be to the detriment of the relationship.

Even when friendships feel as solid as can be, they are still fragile. At any moment, they can be tested, rattled, challenged and even broken. While they can make us feel wonderful, they can also cause misery and heartache. Friendships must be worked at constantly. If we abandon them, or don't put in the effort, we run the risk of derailing everything we've built. This is what makes friendships inherently complex.

LOYALTY AND BETRAYAL

> *"Kaitlyn, let it go. This is something that needs to pass naturally. I'm just her target right now. If we just leave it alone, she'll find someone new. But I'm begging you, if you're really my best friend you'll stay quiet. You can't tell anyone. I mean no one! You have no idea what this is like and it's not your business to fix it."*
>
> **~ Chapter 6, *The Only Way Out***
>
> *I let out a heavy sigh and turned onto my right side, sliding my arm beneath the pillow. My mind shifted back to Rebecca—happy, kind and energetic Rebecca. At least that's the friend I'd known for the last thirteen years. But she's not the girl who came to the coffee shop that night. The girl who walked through those doors just a few hours earlier had a*

certain graveness about her. She appeared somber and subdued and her eyes were tired. Her warming smile and lively spirit were nowhere to be seen. I noticed her shoulders hung low as she slouched in her chair, sinking deep into its wooden frame. I imagine she looked exactly as she felt...damaged. I could feel her heavy heart from where I sat.

Although I was grateful for the fact that Rebecca had opened up to me at least a little, it wasn't enough. I was profoundly worried about her and I feared that over time, matters would only worsen. Our conversation was so brief that I didn't even have a chance to ask her if there had been other incidents between her and Chantel. Even without an answer, my instincts told me there were—and if I was right, this would only further prove my prediction that another encounter was just around the corner. And yet here I lay, still in my bed—a silenced friend. From my perspective, I wasn't a friend at all...far from it, in fact. A real friend would have told someone, spoken out, taken action in some way. But I didn't. As much as I felt the opposing, contradictory pulls of my dilemma deep inside, I was far too afraid to disobey Rebecca's wishes. She'd confided in me that night. Even though it was only for a few minutes and despite the fact that it ended badly, there was still meaning in it. Didn't Rebecca need a friend more than anything else right now? If I turned against her, all trust would be lost. She'd dismiss me the same way she had earlier that morning.

~ **Chapter 7,** *The Only Way Out*

DISCUSSION QUESTIONS

TAKE A MOMENT
What would you do?

1. In the two scenes above, the narrator wants to speak up about a bullying incident but her bullied friend begs her not to. How does this make you feel as the reader?

5. Friendship

2. Why do you think the victimized friend, Rebecca, begs for silence?

_____

_____

_____

3. Do you think the main character (narrator) should tell someone or remain silent and obey her friend's wishes? What would you do in her shoes?

_____

_____

_____

THINGS TO THINK ABOUT

Friendship dynamics can be complicated.

1. When we have close friendships, we value them deeply and we would do anything to keep them.

2. It is possible for the strong feelings we share for our friends to cloud our vision. If we are loyal, we may be inclined to listen to whatever wishes they have, even if they're not the best ones.

3. If we carefully consider our own wants as well as those of our friend, we can determine the right step forward. If there is a discrepancy, it is possible to approach our friend again in different ways or come at the issue from a new angle in order to ultimately make the right move.

Every friendship is dealt a unique hand. Every friendship hand, while different in its own way, also has one card in common: *the loyalty card.* We cannot break our friend's trust and we must remain loyal. This is a key element of friendship.

So then, we come to the crossroads.

- How far will we go to preserve that loyalty?
- Will we do what we believe is "right" even if it means our friend might be upset with us?
- In our minds, does friendship loyalty trump speaking up about something important?
- Are we afraid of losing our friend if we tell someone what is going on with them?

These are all very real questions and completely understandable in scenarios where we find ourselves the bystander of an incident, or a bystander in the sense that we know about someone who may have an issue. We believe they need help, but they think they don't.

There is no right answer and every situation is different.

MOVING FORWARD

Let us try to find ways to confront our situation head on, in an honest, transparent and straightforward manner. The power of genuine and empathetic conversation can go a long way here.

If you're the friend going through something that you don't want others to speak up about, take some time to reflect. Tap into your feelings and thoughts to determine where the block is.

If, on the other hand, you are the friend who wants to speak up and get help but the one directly involved asks you not to, it's time to come at your situation a different way. Think of your friendship and the kind of person your friend is. What might they be feeling right now? Why do you think they are choosing secrecy? Think of new methods of communication that might help you get through.

ACTIONABLE TASKS

1. Define it.

A. What qualities should a good friend <u>not</u> have? Think of a few characteristics that make a bad friend.

CHARACTERISTICS OF A BAD FRIEND
1.
2.
3.

B. What qualities does a good friend have? What qualities do *you* look for in a friend?

QUALITIES THAT MAKE A GOOD FRIEND
1.
2.
3.

2. Pros and cons.

Imagine a scenario where someone has been bullied and does <u>not</u> want to talk about it or report it. A close friend is worried about the bullied person and wants to help by getting all the necessary information and speaking up to take action.

Below, write down all the pros and cons you can think of for each scenario: remaining silent and speaking up.

REMAINING SILENT		SPEAKING UP	
PROS	**CONS**	**PROS**	**CONS**

Can you think of ways to minimize the risks of your "cons" from happening? Describe your ideas.

------

3. Think outside the box.

It's possible for us to approach the situation in a unique way, which may give us better results.

If you're the one pleading for secrecy, deep down you may know this isn't the best way to deal with the situation. At this time, maybe your version of speaking up isn't telling the school principal. Maybe it's confiding in your friend or sports coach. Or maybe you talk to a counselor to gain fresh insights and logical next steps that you're comfortable with.

If you're the one who wants to help and speak up, but you're getting resistance from your friend, take a step back. Consider giving them space for a day or two. After a cooling off period, take them to their favorite place to hang out. Bring it up casually and in a non-threatening way. Offer different ideas of ways you can help. Then, let *them* choose what feels like a good plan. Or write them a note, send an email, or type a quick text or instant message. Most importantly, identify the approach according to your friend's individual personality and traits. Cater to them, not you.

> The complexity of human relationships is never simple to follow; it is like intricate lacework, but lacework made of steel.
> **~ Mignon G. Eberhart**

FEEL

Allow yourself to be real and authentic—whoever that may be. Don't be afraid to be yourself. Connect with people when the opportunity arises. Be true to who you are. Be vulnerable. Treat others well and show that you care. These are the essential elements of genuine friendships.

LEARN

Friendships may come easy, or they may not. These relationships are complex machines that must be maintained and cared for in order to keep running. When it comes to issues of bullying and mental health, the "right move" may not always be crystal clear, so be sure to give the issue careful consideration, keep safety as your guiding star and listen to your gut instincts.

DO

If <u>you</u> need help, find it in yourself to reach out to a friend in whatever way you are most comfortable. If <u>your friend</u> needs help, determine how best to approach the situation. Speak their language and be on their level. Consider the many emotions and feelings they are experiencing. Act in their best interests.

6

SELF-CONFIDENCE

> *"'And now ask yourself, is it really worth it? Whatever thrill you're getting out of the experience now—is it worth a serious injury, the destruction of someone's self-confidence, a suicide or a death?'"*
>
> ~ **Chapter 22,** *The Only Way Out*

In this excerpt, the main character is conducting a presentation in front of her fellow students. She prompts them to think about their potentially bullying behaviors, and the effects of those behaviors on others.

DISCUSSION QUESTIONS

TAKE A MOMENT
Intent versus Impact.

1. Have you ever taken the time to stop and think (*really* think) about the potential effects of your words or actions on another person? Consider a positive and negative scenario.

2. Before you speak, do you consider what you're about to say? Describe a time when you stopped yourself from saying something hurtful or switched your words around in a positive way.

6. Self-Confidence

3. Before you act, do you "think twice"? Describe a time when you did this successfully. How might the outcome have been different if you hadn't "thought twice" about your actions?

THINGS TO THINK ABOUT

How we feel affects how we act.

1. We're all human. In a fleeting moment, considerations, double-checks and second thoughts are sometimes near impossible. Sometimes situations unfold quickly and we make rash decisions. If we're in a poor state of mind, or furthermore, a poor state of self, those fast choices may be reflective of our inner feelings. Just think of how you handle and react to situations when you are happy versus upset, relaxed versus anxious, peaceful versus angry, or overtired versus well-rested. Now imagine that any one of these states is permanent, or at least defines you 90% of the time. In general, if you are upset, anxious, angry and overtired, you are far more likely to speak and act in ways that project those feelings.

2. But now, let us ask ourselves, where do those feelings stem from?

3. If we have an off day, that's one thing. But if this is the way we feel in general, there is a root cause we must address. Self-confidence lies at the core of our being. If we are self-confident, it means we know who we are, we accept who we are, and we live authentically according to who we are.

4. If you love yourself and you feel confident about who you are as a person, do you think you would *go out of your way* to hurt, embarrass or shame another person? If you truly love yourself, do you think you would *allow* someone else to hurt, embarrass or shame you? How likely or unlikely is each scenario?

> *Her hair was long and streaked with a mix of platinum blond and chestnut brown colors in thick, dominant strips. Most other girls' highlights were pencil thin, but the hair on the head directly in front of me made a much bigger statement. It draped over the hood of her beige-colored rain jacket and fell loosely over the sides. It was slightly tangled, as though she'd forgotten to brush it that morning—or, what was likely more accurate, she didn't care. She wore dark blue skinny jeans tucked into black combat-style boots and draped over her left shoulder was a black bag, with the corner of a notebook protruding out of the back corner. Leaning into her left hip with her head tilted, eyes down on her smartphone and right leg extended far out to the side, our confrontational stranger oozed confidence.*
>
> ~ **Chapter 3,** *The Only Way Out*
>
> In the book excerpt above, the girl being described is the one who bullies. Do you think she is genuinely confident in herself? Why or why not?

THE "ACT" OF CONFIDENCE

There are countless studies which show that in the vast majority of bullying cases, those *doing* the bullying suffer in some way. A few of the most common and associated causal links include:

- Stress and trauma (more specifically, a significant situation has occurred in the last five years)
- Aggressive behavior (when communicating or talking through emotions is discouraged, people often turn to aggression)
- Low self-esteem (trying to avoid negative attention on them, deflecting onto others)
- Victim of bullying (research shows that those who have experienced bullying are twice as likely to bully someone else)

- Difficult home life (parents who don't spend enough time, feelings of rejection, violent households)
- Low access to education (lack of understanding about how to treat others)
- Insecure relationships (feeling pressured to do things in order to keep friendships)

So then, would it not be safe to assume that those who bully are *not* confident? They may even be sad, mad or frustrated with their lives. They might be so mentally unwell that they engage in bullying behavior in a desperate attempt to gain power and control of their own lives, by gaining power and control over YOU.

But...they appear to be overflowing with confidence! How?

It may be an "act" they've mastered.

And we all can, too. (*Without* the bullying behavior.)

When we do not engage in bullying behavior, and rather find ourselves struggling with our own personal self-confidence, either in general or as a direct result of past trauma or victimization, we too can "act" confident. Simultaneously, on our own time, we can work on and build our self-confidence from within. We can give more attention to the parts of ourselves and our lives that need care, which in turn, can help us foster a sustainable, confident new way of life.

EXUDING CONFIDENCE—EVEN WHEN WE DON'T *FEEL* CONFIDENT

Have you ever heard the line, "fake it till you make it?" In relation to self-confidence, the idea behind this is that by imitating confidence, competence and an optimistic mindset, we can eventually realize all of these qualities in our lives, and therefore, achieve the results we're striving for. If there is truth behind this well-known saying, then it *is* possible to come across as confident even when we're not. Simultaneously, if these outward actions are coupled with inward actions to build inner strength, then we can one day truly live in full confidence and reap the benefits of a confident life.

Now that we know bullying behavior seeks to bring the perpetrator a sense of control over someone else, one of the best things we can do is exude confidence wherever we go—even if we have to "fake it" temporarily.

Here are a few physical tips on how we can do this:

- Make eye contact
- Stand up tall and straight
- Lower your tone of voice (no high-pitched, shrill sounds)
- Speak slowly and clearly
- Allow for silences
- Breathe long and deep (avoid short, quick breaths)
- Use your hands when you talk
- Avoid fidgeting
- Take big steps when you walk

BEING OUR AUTHENTIC SELVES

Our tween and adolescent years are much about finding ourselves. It may come relatively easy for some, and may be a more difficult process for others. Whatever our path and whatever our journey, it is important that we allow ourselves the time we need to grow into our true selves.

Ask yourself:

What are my interests?

What do I believe in?

------

6. Self-Confidence

What are my personal values?

What matters most to me?

What am I passionate about?

What's my sense of style?

What are my priorities?

When our stage of life is one in which we are exposed to many different people, opinions, options and directions, it is not uncommon to feel lost at times. Are we comfy or fancy dressers? Do we like ball caps or headbands? Do we like to be funny, or are we more of the serious type? Are we more inclined towards sports or the arts? Do we enjoy being social or do we prefer to spend time alone? It can take years to settle in to who we really are. Even then, as we grow and evolve as individuals, we can change our minds, make alterations in our behavior, switch our priorities or develop fresh curiosities that we are eager to explore.

Whether it's how we look, what we're interested in, the process of identifying our passions, or understanding what really matters to us as individuals, we must always bear in mind that how long it takes doesn't matter. We can give ourselves the time we need and experiment however we like. And even that is no guarantee that we will figure it all out—we might not. Our personal development and evolution take place over the course of our entire lives. Given that this is so, what matters most is determining who we want to be at *this* time. Right here, right now. And then, we must live it. Be it. Love it. Have confidence in it.

Our true authentic self is who we are.

Of course, there is always the risk that our authentic self may be rejected by some. This must, however, be a risk we are willing to take because even if we try to be someone we're not, the same level of risk still applies. So, we might as well spend our time being exactly who we are.

> The only thing that matters in life is your own opinion about yourself.
> **~ Osho**

CHOOSING WHERE WE WANT TO BE

We all have choices to make. When it comes to who we spend time with, what we do and where we are, it's up to us to decide. One of the simplest and best ways to build our self-confidence is to put ourselves in situations that make us feel good.

For example, discover what you're good at. Ask yourself, "How do I want to spend my spare time? What am I interested in? What do I like to do?" It might be soccer, dance, hockey, painting, building, gardening, writing, math or coding. See where your talents lie and carve out blocks of time to do what you love. When you spend time doing something you're good at and passionate about, you also *feel* great doing it.

When it comes to our personal time and the way in which we live our lives, it's up to us to maximize and optimize. In other words, we must surround ourselves with people who accept us for who we are. We must put ourselves in situations that make us feel good. And we must do the things that make us happy. If we can find ways to incorporate more of this into our lives, and if we can commit to working on loving and accepting our genuine selves, it's only a matter of time before those positive feelings compound and grow into sustainable self-confidence that proves we no longer need to fake it because we've made it.

WE'RE WORTH IT

There may be times when we find ourselves in questionable situations.

Was that friend's comment on social media really a joke, or was there some offensive truth behind it?

Our friends constantly call us names but then immediately follow up with, "Oh, don't take things so seriously! I'm just kidding around...we're friends."

We're confronted by bullying behavior, but don't want to make a big deal of it so we brush it off like it's nothing.

The thing is, it's *something*.

Instead of just taking it in stride, re-think, re-evaluate and take a cold, hard look at the situation. If someone isn't making you feel good or is causing you mental or physical pain of some kind, that's not okay. No matter how seemingly small or insignificant, negative situations have a tendency to continue and mount if they are not addressed *immediately*. If something doesn't *feel* right, it *isn't* right.

If speaking up is required, *you deserve to say the words*.
If standing up for yourself is needed, *do it for you*.
If action is needed, take it because *you're worth it*.

MOVING FORWARD

> To fall in love with yourself is the first secret to happiness.
> **~ Robert Morely**

However old we are, whatever phase of life we are in, let us remember that the confidence and love we have for ourselves is forever evolving. We are different versions of ourselves now than one, five, ten years ago. And we will likely be different versions of ourselves one, five, ten years from today. This is life. This is the process. We love ourselves in various ways as time passes. Maybe we'll discover a new talent we're proud of. Or perhaps we'll dye our hair and feel gorgeous in our new locks. We might start working out and fall in love with our fresh muscular stature, or turn our love of baking into an entrepreneurial dream!

Take time for you. More specifically, take time to make *you* the very best version of yourself that you can be.

6. Self-Confidence

ACTIONABLE TASKS

1. Map it out.

Grab a pen or pencil, and the following three colored pencils, crayons or markers: red, yellow and green.

The circles below represent several areas of your life. It's not everything, but it's a few of the most important. Go through each circle, one by one. Set a timer for 60 seconds for each circle. In that 60 seconds, think about the particular area of your life. Allow your mind to ponder, analyze and evaluate. Ask yourself, "Overall, how do I feel about this part of my life?"

Green = Good to Great
Yellow = Satisfied to Okay
Red = Bad to Terrible

Color in each circle according to how you feel about it, following the legend above. For simplicity and visual impact, there are only three colors for you to choose from. Naturally, you may find there are some circles that don't perfectly fit just one color. If you're stuck, feel free to use up to two colors in your circles (either green and yellow, which symbolizes somewhere in between "okay and good," or red and yellow, which represents a feeling somewhere in between "okay and bad"). You cannot have a circle with all three colors, nor can you have a circle with opposing colors, green and red.

FRIENDS	FAMILY	SCHOOL	EXTRA-CURRICULARS
◯	◯	◯	◯
FUN	LOVE	HEALTH	SELF-ESTEEM
◯	◯	◯	◯

Once you have taken 60 seconds to think about each circle, and you've colored them all in, reset your timer to two minutes. Take this time to look at all the circles on your page. Do you see a lot of green? Yellow? Red? Is there a mix of all the colors, or do you notice one color is predominant?

This exercise is designed to give you a visual snapshot of how you feel about eight areas of your life. What your colored circles reveal may be able to show you which facets need more of your attention.

2. Make moves.

> If you don't like something change it. If you can't change it, change your attitude.
> **~ Maya Angelou**

There are always areas for improvement. Each and every one of us is on a lifelong process of personal development—that is, if we choose to accept the challenge. What's most important is this: at any stage of our lives, if we are unhappy about something, we have the power and the right to change it. Yes, it takes effort and work on our part, but life is far too short simply to sit back and accept our unhappiness and dissatisfaction. So, take a look at those circles again and then write your answers to the following questions.

A. Are any of your circles red? If yes, why? Can you name the specific things that are bothering you?

B. Are any of your circles yellow? If yes, why? What are the reasons behind your feelings being dragged down from green to yellow in these areas of your life?

C. Are all of your circles green? If yes, congratulations! That's fantastic. On the other hand, there's no such thing as perfect, so what do you think you can do to keep them green?

D. For one of your red circles that you evaluated the lowest, write down three small things you could do over the next week to start improving that color.

(For example: Tell your friend you don't like it when they call you that nickname because it's hurtful. Wake up 30 minutes earlier every day so you can paint. Enroll yourself in a music class. Ask your family if you can eat more dinners together. Do one YouTube exercise video a day. Ask your teacher for extra help in math. Tell yourself you're awesome every morning.)

---

3. Write a resume intro.

Imagine you are applying for a job you really want. At the very top of most resumes, there is a section called "Profile" or "Highlights" or "Summary." It is a small paragraph consisting of one to three sentences that call out your experience, qualities and skills. It should answer the question, "Why hire this person?" This is an excellent confidence-boosting exercise because it makes you describe yourself in the most positive and successful way possible.

Write a sample resume profile below.

----

4. Affirmations.

Never underestimate the power of the words you use *with yourself*.

Consider individual power verbs that drive you towards positive actions. For example:

- Act
- Command
- Advocate
- Achieve
- Do
- Grow
- Initiate

6. Self-Confidence

One of the best things we can do for our personal self-esteem is tell ourselves what we need to hear!

"There's no one else quite like me on this Earth."
"I owe it to myself, to be myself."
"I am incredible in my own way, inside and out."
"Happiness is an attitude."
"I am worth it."
"I am stronger than I think."
"I am capable of doing whatever I put my mind to."
"I am beautiful."
"I am ME."

> CONFIDENCE is not 'they will like me'.
> CONFIDENCE is 'I'll be fine if they don't'.
> ~ Christina Grimmie

FEEL

It's okay to feel unsure of ourselves sometimes, and we may not always be living life on "Cloud Nine" (which means, in a state of bliss and elated happiness). What's important is <u>that most of the time</u>, generally speaking, during the majority of our days we feel happy, satisfied and good about who we are.

LEARN

Outwardly, it is possible to act confident and self-assured even when we aren't. There are simple tactics we can use to exude the kind of confidence that makes us impermeable to bullying behaviors and victimization. Internally, whatever we are dissatisfied with in our lives or about ourselves, if it is changeable, then we have the power to change it. Putting in the time and the work is all that is standing between low self-esteem and high self-esteem.

DO

Take action. Start trying out the tactics you've learned in this section. Give yourself the time you deserve. Evaluate the different areas of your life to see where you feel good and where you need to put in a little extra work. Make a list of small things you can start doing right now, to work on YOU as you continually build your self-confidence and live every day as your true self.

7

DEALING WITH THE AFTERMATH

Devoid of energy, emotion and purpose, I was just another girl with a broken heart. I could barely even recognize myself. Once a strong, willful and vibrant personality, I was an effervescent girl who could never get enough of the socialite lifestyle. Being alone was out of the question before. I'd accept the company of others any day, any moment before I'd sit alone. And now? The polar opposite. A lost soul. A forlorn teenager. In those darkest days, the world had me conquered. How could anyone expect me to beat this? All my confidence, all my determination, all my gusto...I'd lost it somewhere along the way. I had not an ounce of faith in my ability to overcome this hardship. It was taking me, consuming me, one cell at a time.

~ **Chapter 17**, *The Only Way Out*

My parents played music from the sixties at just the right volume for me to enjoy the background tunes, and let my mind immerse itself in a sea of transformational thoughts. At first, there was a period of realization. What I just did was speak up. Exactly what I should have done for Rebecca, but didn't.

I messed up. I should have told someone. I messed up. I should have told someone. The profound words echoed in my head. While I did feel fresh guilt and shame, my mind was in a completely different place. I started to ask myself, So what? So what? What are you going to do about it NOW?

....

My energy began to rise further and further in the back seat of the car that day. Mind racing and my heart beating faster and faster by the minute, I knew I was on the brink of something big—something huge. Although my secret truths were painful to admit, they had the ability to give other people a perspective that no book, movie or classroom lesson ever could.

That was it!
My new-found purpose.
Rebecca's story needed to be told. And I would be the one to tell it.

~ **Chapter 18**, *The Only Way Out*

7. Dealing with the Aftermath

DISCUSSION QUESTIONS

TAKE A MOMENT
Dissect it.

1. What are the key differences between the excerpt from Chapter 17 and the excerpt from Chapter 19?

2. How are the main character's feelings in Chapter 17 different from Chapter 19?

3. Have you ever found yourself in a state of mind that changes and evolves as you deal with the aftermath of a situation? Describe what you experienced.

> ### THINGS TO THINK ABOUT
>
> *Action is key.*
>
> 1. In the first book excerpt, we are invited into the mind of a young person who is struggling deeply with a tragic circumstance that has unfolded. She feels utterly hopeless and her thoughts are predominantly focused on *what happened* and how she won't be able to move on from it. Even though they are natural, and we must always allow ourselves to process our feelings after any adverse event, it is important to recognize that these thoughts are unproductive and negative. When it comes to moving on and moving forward, they won't do us any good.
>
> 2. In the second excerpt, the inner dialogue feels as though it is completely opposite to the first. The same girl's thoughts have transformed and turned around to face the opposite direction—the direction of *forward* not *backward*. In other words, *what's next?* Or, as she asks herself in the book, *"So what?"* Instead of allowing her mind to continue to be preoccupied with thoughts of past events, she digs inward and begins to carve a productive path for herself moving forward, no matter how difficult it may be.

WHEN SOMETHING HAPPENS

When something happens…what do we do next?

That "something" could be anything. It could be small or big, minor or major, a little harsh or extremely traumatic, easy to get over or life changing. *What* it is, doesn't matter nearly as much as *what happens after*.

Once something happens, it is done. It has already taken place and there is absolutely nothing anyone can do about it. Part of the past now, it is unchangeable. What *is* still changeable however, is everything that happens next.

Consider this:

> *What's done is done. Let us not focus on what has already happened, but rather on what we're going to do next. We can have an impact only on what is to come, not what already came. And in the event that we are to blame, we must ask ourselves an important question: what are we going to do differently next time?*

This is powerful for two reasons.

1. It grounds us. It reassures us in the sense that it makes us recognize the fact that no one is perfect, and this life we're living is not perfect. Bad things are going to happen and we ourselves are going to mess up.
2. It gives us hope. It trains our brains to think and behave productively, not negatively. It discourages wallowing and stewing for too long. And it invites us to consider a change in the way we act so that we may improve the situation or do better next time.

GO THROUGH THE MOTIONS

In the aftermath of a situation where you were directly or indirectly involved, the feelings, experiences and reactions may be mild, moderate or severe. Whatever the level of your emotions, it is important to allow yourself, with complete wholeheartedness, to *feel* what you are feeling and to *experience* what you are going through.

One of the worst things we can do is deny, bottle up, push down and set aside our emotions surrounding the event. This has the potential to damage our mental health and set us back in some way later in life.

There's a reason why we feel certain emotions or experience particular struggles in our lives after an adverse situation. It's okay that we feel this way. It's okay that we're struggling.

Sometimes…

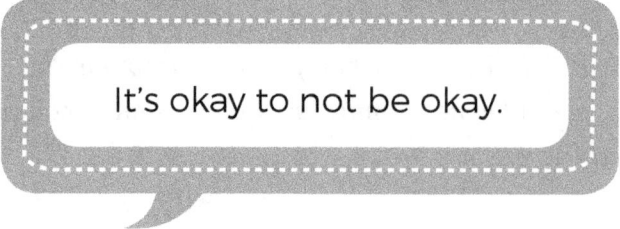

What we can do from here is figure out meaningful and useful methods to use as we go through different stages of emotion and struggle.

MOVING FORWARD

Aftermath is defined as the consequences or effects of an unpleasant, significant event. "Unpleasant" and "significant" are two defining adjectives that mean different things to different people. Our idea of an unpleasant and significant event might be getting into an argument with our closest friend. Or it could be dealing with the separation of our parents. Or being bullied. Or finding out that one of our classmates has been diagnosed with a mental illness.

Any event can have an aftermath. If something has happened and we find ourselves troubled afterwards, then we need to pay attention to what we're going through.

ACTIONABLE TASKS

As you take time to deal with what has happened, here are a few tactics to get you started on the right foot as you travel down your path to recovery:

1. Create a safe space.

A safe space might be your bedroom. Or the hammock in your backyard. Or sitting in the family room with your parents. Or being at gymnastics. Or shooting the puck on the ice. When we find ourselves overwhelmed with emotion or struggling to process new developments, we can go to our safe space. Instantly, this gives us a sense of comfort. And when we feel it, we are better able to return to a state of calm and think logically about our situation.

What setting makes you feel safe in your life? Describe it.

------

2. Perform calming activities.

A calming activity can be anything that puts you at ease. A little bit of anxiousness or nervousness within our bodies is okay. Our heartrate may quicken and our breathing might speed up. If, however, this state becomes perpetual, constant or excessive, this can have negative effects on our sleep, decision-making abilities and long-term health. By engaging in calming activities, we can successfully manage and combat this, continually restoring our body to its resting state. We each have our own ideas of what a calming activity is in our lives. Listening to music. Watching a great movie. Doing Yoga. Hot Yoga. Meditation. Writing in our journal. Cooking. Baking. Bike riding. Dancing. Working out. Sketching. Painting. Calling a friend.

What activities make you feel calm? Describe them.

------

3. Connect.

Human beings need other human beings. As you work through the aftermath of whatever situation you have experienced, it's more important than ever before that you connect with others. Talk to your parents. Watch a movie with your siblings. Have a friend over for dinner. Schedule an appointment with a therapist. Open up and get it out. Let yourself be vulnerable. The more you connect with the people in your life, the more you allow yourself to heal, move on in a healthy way, and most importantly, be happy.

List three people who you enjoy spending time with and who you know will make you feel good, even during tough times.

------

4. Make a plan.

You know yourself better than anyone else does. Take the time to figure out what you need during this time and then put together a plan of action. That might look like a weekly appointment with a therapist, a few friend hangouts, dinner as a family every day after school and plugged-in time for meditation each night before bed. Or maybe you determine that you want to sign up for a gym membership so you can work out a few times a week, or you bake muffins every Sunday for the week.

What would your recovery plan look like? Write down a few ideas.

> When something happens to you, you have two choices in how to deal with it. You can either get bitter, or get better.
> **~ Benjamin Disraeli**

7. Dealing with the Aftermath

FEEL

Whatever we've been through, it's okay to feel all the emotions and repercussions associated with that event. In fact, if we don't allow ourselves to feel them now, they may very well bring us down and hold us back later.

LEARN

Personal development and nurturing are ongoing processes. There is no such thing as perfection. As we travel through life and experience different phases, we are continually changing and evolving. After an adverse event, it's about figuring out what we need to heal, learn and move on.

DO

Once you determine what you need in order to make it through to the other side, DO IT. Make a plan and stick to it. Show yourself grace and understanding. Create time for exactly what you need. There are no right and wrong answers, just stay the course.

SUPPORT CREW

> *I couldn't have asked for a better reaction from my parents. While I could tell they were severely disappointed and expected more out of their daughter in such a situation, their compassion, understanding and sympathy shone through. They made me painfully regret the fact that I hadn't told them sooner.*
>
> *....*
>
> *Even though there were uncomfortable and serious conversations, what I remember about that car ride home was our empowering, future-focused dialogue. I think Mom and Dad understood that forward talk would be much more beneficial than backward reflection, for which there would be plenty of times to speak but now wasn't one of them. We planned, we discussed, we brainstormed and we bounced ideas off one another.*
>
> **~ Chapter 19, *The Only Way Out***

In the book excerpts above, what we can undoubtedly take away from the main character's words is this: her mother and father give her wholehearted support. She has told them something that was not only difficult for her to express, but also difficult for her parents to hear. And yet, what do they do? They support her. They make sure she knows they are 100% there for her. They propel the conversations forward, not backward.

These are the marks of an excellent support network. Do you have one?

DISCUSSION QUESTIONS

TAKE A MOMENT
Ask yourself.

1. If you had a difficult thing to share, who would you tell?

2. How do you think that person (or people) would react?

_____

_____

_____

_____

3. Do you believe you have a strong support network in your life? If yes, who is in it?

_____

_____

_____

THINGS TO THINK ABOUT

Getting what you need.

1. It is a scientifically proven fact that humans need social and emotional support from other humans. According to the Canadian Mental Health Association, social and emotional connection "...can lower anxiety and depression, help us regulate our emotions, lead to higher self-esteem and empathy, and actually improve our immune systems."

2. If we neglect or deny our human need to connect with others, we are simultaneously putting our personal health at risk.

3. When we connect, we build relationships. Solid relationships are grounded in support for one another.

WHAT IS A SUPPORT NETWORK?

A support network is a group of people that helps you achieve your goals—personal, academic, and eventually professional goals. They're the people in our lives on which we can depend and rely. We share common interests and values with them. We trust each other. We spend time, share laughs and love lots. We feel good around one another. We give advice and offer guidance. We congratulate one another on tasks well done. We go through triumphs and tragedies together. We talk, but we listen more. When one of us falls, we lift them up. And if one of us is soaring high, we fly along with them.

The people in our support network are the ones with whom we feel the happiest and most fulfilled. They can be our parents, relatives, friends, teammates, teachers, coaches, guidance counselors and therapists. Who they are doesn't matter—it's about who they are *to you* that counts.

WHY DO WE NEED A SUPPORT NETWORK?

We need a group of support people in our lives for a number of reasons. When you mess up, who's there for you? When you're sad, who makes you smile? When you're mad, who lets you vent? When you're worried or afraid, who listens closely and offers up solutions?

Perhaps it's possible to go through all the trials, tribulations and triumphs this world has to offer by ourselves. Maybe we can choose to be alone. But what fun would that be—and is it even wise to live this way?

When we have a strong support network that goes along for the ride with us, we benefit from:

- Improved ability to cope with adverse situations
- Alleviated emotional stress
- Promotion of lifelong, strong mental health
- Increased self-esteem
- Lowered cardiovascular risk (i.e., blood pressure)

WHAT IF WE DON'T HAVE A NETWORK?

If we feel as though we're lacking a strong support network in our lives, it's quite possible that we are experiencing a number of negative effects:

- Loneliness
- Anxiety
- Depression
- Cardiovascular risks
- Poor sleep
- Unhealthy behaviors

We all like to be alone sometimes—even the most extreme extroverts. Having said that, we also *need* human connection at times and it feels especially good to know that we have people in our lives who are always there for us no matter what, and who we also feel comfortable telling "Hey, I really need to be on my own for a bit right now."

Feeling as though we don't have anyone we can turn to is problematic. Even for those of us who *do* have people to turn to, sometimes they don't give us the amount of emotional support we need. We would do better with more. In both scenarios, there are things we can do either to build a good support network, or strengthen our existing one.

MOVING FORWARD

Do you have a personal support network in your life?
If yes, how would you rate your support crew from 1 (weak) to 10 (strong)?

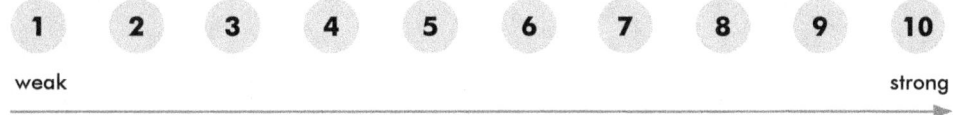

Acknowledging and understanding the importance of having a solid support network is the first step. During moments of frustration it can be both tempting and quite easy to stand up and proclaim, "I don't need anyone! I can do it alone!" This may work quite well—temporarily. There will, however, come a time when the loneliness sets in, and we begin to feel lost and forsaken. When we shut ourselves off from developing connections with the people and the world around us, we run the risk of doing ourselves a considerable amount of harm.

Humans need humans. Instead of trying to do it alone, what we really ought to do is figure out how to live meaningful lives in connection with others. Not every connection will be profound and life-changing, but it will be present and you will be connected nonetheless. Beyond that, we can work towards acquiring and building a support network of people we truly resonate with, share common values with, like to spend time with, can tell anything to, can confide in, and with whom we can be happy and fulfilled.

ACTIONABLE TASKS

1. Your contribution.

Studies show that relationships are not created out of a need, but rather as a result of sharing gifts, experiences, interests and skills, which in turn, develop *meaningful connections*.

1. **Make a list of five things you have to contribute.** (Tip: keep your list general—i.e. funny jokes, sense of humor, fun, positivity, empathy, good listening abilities, deep insights, knowledge.)

    1. _____
    2. _____
    3. _____
    4. _____
    5. _____

2. **Create a list of contributions you can make, according to three different groups of people in your life.** (Tip: think of the different areas of your life. Your contributions in one area are likely to differ from your contributions in another. For example: school, home, extended family, gymnastics class, music lesson, lacrosse team).

Group #1: _____

- _____
- _____
- _____

Group #2: _____

- _____
- _____
- _____

Group #3: _____

- _____
- _____
- _____

2. Get out there.

When we feel as though we haven't yet found a group of individuals who we can really call our support network then it's time for us to be more proactive in finding them. For example, maybe making friends at school isn't the easiest, but we're getting along well with people in our extracurricular activities. Or perhaps the people in our sports class aren't who we want to spend more time with, but we're making great friends at our new job.

Here are a few ideas of how you can meet more people and begin building solid relationships. You'll never know unless you get out there and try.

A. **Start close to home.** Turn to your family members. Parents, siblings, grandparents, relatives and cousins. A close-knit family can be one of the most incredible sources of support for us at every age. In most cases, family members want us to succeed and are there to offer love, time and advice unquestionably.

B. **Walk your street.** You may be surprised to find friendly neighbors in close proximity to where you live! Talk a walk. Step outside after dinner. Be present in your neighbourhood. You never know who you might meet, or what friend might introduce you to a friend of theirs, and so on.

C. **Explore your school.** Maybe you have a great circle of friends in different classes and who you spend time with during spare periods and outside of school hours. But if you feel as though you haven't yet made solid connections, look beyond your current group. Introduce yourself or spark up a conversation with someone new (it's only awkward for the first few seconds). Consider joining a club or society, go to school events, or try out for one of the athletic teams. By expanding your touch points, you build additional relationships and can start forming a great support network.

D. **Get a part-time job.** (If you're old enough and able to without compromising your academics or extracurricular obligations.) In any new position, you'll meet different people and will have an opportunity to build connections.

E. **Be active in your community.** Look into local groups in your areas of interest or volunteer your time at a local food bank, charitable organization or social service center. The more you participate in the world around you, the more people you'll meet and the greater your sense of personal fulfillment will be.

3. Work at it and don't neglect it.

The more we put into something, the more we get out of it. Relationships are just the same. We cannot expect to be a world-class soccer player without practicing, the same way we cannot expect to have a deep, meaningful relationship without putting time and effort into that person. Relationships require our nurturing attention. Without this, they can fall apart with ease, just like a learned language is quickly forgotten if not spoken on a regular basis.

Working at a relationship that is important to you might look something like this:

- You maintain an emotional connection
- You confide in your person
- You offer support when needed
- You are open and honest
- You show them you care
- You are committed to spending time together
- You are proactive about reaching out and making contact (spending time together, messages, chats, emails, phone calls)

> You can't achieve anything entirely by yourself. There's a support system that is a basic requirement of human existence. To be happy and successful on earth, you just have to have people that you rely on.
> ~ **Michael Schur**

FEEL

As human beings, we need to <u>feel</u> connected to others. This is ingrained in our very nature. We must allow ourselves to feel real and vulnerable with the people around us so that we may form beautiful relationships that support and fulfill us.

LEARN

Every now and then, it's a good idea to look at our lives and evaluate. Do we have a solid support crew around us? Are we lacking meaningful relationships? Would it benefit us to work on our existing relationships, form new ones, or both?

DO

If the relationships are there but are not fulfilling enough, then we must put in the time and effort they need to grow. If we haven't yet found a solid support network, then we must do everything in our control to get out there and find it. Then the real building can begin.

9

ALL THE WAYS UP START WITH TALKING

"Oh, Rebecca!" It broke my heart—hearing her account of the incident as I tried, somehow, to understand what she was going through. But I knew I couldn't—and she did too. The hurt, the frustration, the humiliation—it was overwhelming even to think about, let alone experience. Relieved she told me, but afraid only the wrong words would come out of my mouth, I stayed silent. I wanted to cry too, but I knew it was best to stay strong.

After a few minutes, I said sternly, "When do you want to tell your parents?"

Rebecca's eyes widened. "No way," she responded firmly, "Kaitlyn, I'm serious. No matter what, you cannot tell them."

"What!?" I couldn't believe what I was hearing. "Why?"

Her tone was now condescending and offensive. "You really don't get it, do you?" I felt my cheeks turn crimson red.

"If I tell my parents, they'll march into that school, talk to the principal, and embarrass the hell out of me! I don't need to solve this—I need to forget it ever happened. What do you think they'll honestly do to Chantel? Give her detention? Suspend her? They're not going to expel her...not a single teacher saw what happened! She'll find out my parents did this and come after me even harder. Is that what you want?"

"Obviously not, Rebecca, but we have to do something!"

"Kaitlyn, let it go. This is something that needs to pass naturally. I'm just her target right now. If we just leave it alone, she'll find someone new. But I'm begging you, if you're really my best friend you'll stay quiet. You can't tell anyone. I mean no one! You have no idea what this is like and it's not your business to fix it."

"But I want to tell our parents <u>because</u> you're my best friend!" I exclaimed. "You just want me to sit back and do nothing? I can't. It's not right. Marcel saw what happened yesterday, you know, and he filed a report with one of the guidance counselors."

~ Chapter 6, *The Only Way Out*

This excerpt illustrates one form of <u>talking</u>. A concerned friend finds out about a bullying incident that occurred and takes it upon herself to confront her victimized best friend and offer support.

9. All the Ways Up Start with Talking

DISCUSSION QUESTIONS

TAKE A MOMENT
Think about the possibilities.

1. In this scene, do you think someone is right and someone is wrong? Why or why not?

2. Is it possible that both characters are right? Why or why not?

3. What do you think you might do next if you were the main character? What do you think you might do next if you were the victimized friend?

> ### THINGS TO THINK ABOUT
>
> *It's not always simple.*
>
> 1. Just because talking and speaking up can be described as "the right things to do," doesn't mean they are easy, nor does it mean that the victimized person is wrong in their resistance.
>
> 2. Talking and speaking up must always take place with safety in mind. The safety of everyone involved must be carefully considered to ensure that no greater danger will arise, and that the people who need help receive it quickly.
>
> 3. Think of talking and speaking up as positive actions. In order to be positive, these actions must consider everyone's wellbeing. Will talking help? Will speaking up create change? Can communication be used to make a positive difference in someone's life?

WHY TALK?

TALKING is COMMUNICATION.

COMMUNICATION is HUMAN CONNECTION.

And we all want it. In fact, we all *need* it.

It is a core psychological need that is essential to our mental health, our overall satisfaction in life and our sense of wellbeing.

To connect, we must see and interact with others.

We need to TALK.

9. All the Ways Up Start with Talking

Open and honest talking...

> Builds trust.
> Fosters genuine relationships.
> Bridges the gap between us.

Did you know that there are real, proven benefits to talking?

1. **It brings relief.**
   Talking is a release of what you're feeling inside. By talking openly about what you are feeling or experiencing, you are letting it out into the open. Picture a rechargeable battery like the one in your phone or watch. When it's fully charged, its energy is at maximum capacity, but then as you start using it, the energy diminishes and the charge decreases. Now think of yourself as the rechargeable battery. If you are charged with feelings of sadness, fear, anxiousness or anger, when you talk about it you are no longer bottling it in. Those energies get expended and released, putting you more at ease with less charge.

2. **It makes you feel better.**
   Just the simple act of talking lets you get stuff off your chest. If something is bothering you, why deal with it alone? When you make the decision to tell someone else about it, you instantly feel better. For example, you witnessed something that was wrong. You believe your friend might be going through a troubling time. You were cruel to someone else. Your mind doesn't feel quite right these days. Find a person you trust and talk it over: release those thoughts.

3. **It leads to new solutions.**
   Talking out loud is like magic. Do it with yourself, or with a person of your choosing. By talking out loud, you think of new ways forward. It happens naturally. Things make sense when they didn't before. If you're talking with another person, they may have fresh insights and different perspectives you haven't even considered.

4. **It works by yourself, too.**
   Often, simply the sound of your own voice talking about whatever is on your mind helps tremendously. If you're not quite ready to talk to someone else yet, have no fear. Talk to

yourself. Come to terms with what you're going through. Recognize negative thoughts. Reframe your thinking. If you change the way you think, you can change the way you live.

TALKING TO SOMEONE WHO NEEDS HELP

If we have a friend who has experienced something traumatic, or we know someone who is currently going through an adverse time in their life, there may come a moment when we realize they could benefit from an open conversation. Before we approach them, it's a good idea to consider their personality, think about how they might want to be spoken to, and put ourselves in their shoes to gain insight into the thoughts, feelings and emotions they might be experiencing.

We ought to be prepared for what could be an easy and comfortable conversation, or an awkward and uncomfortable one. If your friend denies or pushes back, follow your gut instincts. You can table the conversation for tomorrow. Or show your friend support in other ways like a hug, funny text or a movie one night after school. Come at the situation a different way and see what they might be receptive to. Remember, we're all different. Bottom line: don't give up. If you think the situation is serious, tell someone of authority who can help further.

What is most important to keep in mind is the fact that we are doing something good. By reaching out and offering our helping hand to someone, even if they don't respond favorably at first, deep down they are likely to feel thankful that someone cares enough to offer their helping hand. This can have a greater impact than you might think.

TALKING TO SOMEONE WHEN <u>YOU</u> NEED HELP

Maybe something terrible happened to us. Maybe we were victimized. Or maybe it has become very apparent that we are struggling mentally.

On the other hand, needing help isn't always so clear. Maybe nothing happened to us, but we think we may have witnessed something unacceptable. Maybe we don't think we were victimized but someone treated us badly and we're not yet fully seeing it for what it is. Or maybe we're experiencing mild mental issues such as perpetual negative thoughts, anxiety or trouble sleeping, but so far we've brushed them off as nothing and only now are we considering a talk with someone about it.

Whatever the situation, we must constantly remind ourselves that it is *never* wrong to speak up and talk about it. Talking openly can lead to beautiful solutions we didn't think were possible. We must find the courage to pick our person or group of people, and come out with whatever is on our mind. If who we choose cannot deal with what we tell them, that doesn't mean it was wrong to speak up, but rather that we need to find someone else. If that "someone else" isn't in our immediate circle, we can turn to the professionals in our lives such as teachers, guidance counselors, coaches, mentors, doctors and psychologists.

MOVING FORWARD

Talking isn't everything. It doesn't solve every problem or make all issues disappear. This is not its purpose. Rather, talking is a necessary step toward the solution. It is the means through which we can gain relief, arrive at resolutions and discover the best path forward. It is a stepping stone in our journey.

Human beings have the ability to talk and communicate like no other species in the world. When we decide to talk, we are putting our most powerful tool to great use. As we talk, we build trust, we foster and maintain genuine relationships that are good for our overall wellbeing, and we naturally bridge the gap between ourselves and the people around us.

Making the conscious decision to talk (about anything and everything) is not only about helping someone in need or "doing what's right." It's also about our own personal happiness. And we all deserve to be happy.

Words may not be the full solution in many a circumstance, but *talking* is the first step. Without it, no greater meaningful change can take place.

Talking is *the way out* if you are...

- Being bullied
- Bullying another person
- Struggling with something inside
- Noticing a friend in trouble

Talking openly and speaking up isn't always easy. In fact, it can be extremely difficult. As you channel your inner super hero to bring your brave and courageous self to the forefront, keep this in mind:

> It isn't WHAT you say that matters, but rather that you simply SAY IT.
> ~ Katie Kuperman

ACTIONABLE TASKS

1. Make a list.

Write down the names of three people in your life who you feel safe and comfortable talking to. Remember, these people can be anyone. This list is only for your eyes so there is no risk of judgement or misunderstanding. (Consider: parent, relative, friend, colleague, boss, coach, doctor, therapist, guidance counselor, even the technician at the veterinary clinic or the cashier at the grocery store.)

1. _____
2. _____
3. _____

2. Review.

Take a look at the people on your list from #1. Are you surprised about any of the names on it? Now, number the names on the list in order of preference and priority. Who would you want to speak with first? If they aren't easily accessible, who would you turn to next? Jot down a few notes about each name on your list if there are different reasons why you might speak to each person. For example, you might choose a friend to talk with about romantic relationship troubles, but you might prefer your mom for something that's bothering you physically or mentally.

#1 Priority: _____

#2 Priority: _____

#3 Priority: _____

3. Get comfortable.

Get comfortable with how you feel inside—no matter what that is. How you feel is how you feel. We cannot always control it. Particularly if we're struggling in some way, often times our go-to reaction is "I have to fix this! I need to change the way I feel inside" when really what's best is to allow ourselves to *feel*, to process and to let it be.

4. Know and trust how good you will feel after you speak up.

Now we know the benefits associated with talking openly, one of which is relief. If you're hesitant and dreading the process of talking openly, focus on the positives after you've gotten it off your chest.

5. Begin with someone you know and trust.

We all have at least one person—and if we don't, then it's time to turn to a professional (teacher, doctor, therapist, helpline). Choose your best path and press forward.

6. Don't worry about what will happen next.

Often we block ourselves from vocalizing what we're going through or how we're feeling because we're afraid of what might happen after. Will our trusted person judge us? Look at us differently? Go into a state of shock? Run away? There's a famous quote from Mark Twain and it goes like this:

> I've had a lot of worries in my life, most of which never happened.
> ~ Mark Twain

In other words, the human mind has a tendency to worry about potential outcomes. Since those outcomes have not yet come true and because we have no way of knowing for certain if they will, we must make a conscious effort to control and dissipate those worries. If by chance, something bad does happen after we talk, we will deal with it at that time.

7. Say what's on your mind—or write it if you can't yet say it.

Journal, write bullet points, keep a diary, make sticky notes—the form doesn't matter. If you're not yet comfortable with the idea of talking to someone, write your thoughts down on a piece of paper. A study by the American Psychology Association showed that writing can help to relieve stress by combatting intrusive and negative thoughts. By writing about negative experiences, the study explains that people can overcome them by putting things into perspective and concentrating on the positives.

8. Practice.

Do self-rehearsal. If you feel nervous about talking openly or speaking up about something, practice it in your mind first. Then say it out loud by yourself, or rehearse in front of a mirror.

Consider videotaping yourself and playing it back afterwards so you can see how you come across. Each of these methods can help you gain confidence and get your desired message across.

9. Be honest about *why* you're struggling.

There's no shame. We all struggle with things from time to time. Honesty, openness and vulnerability are what keep us connected as human beings. In hard times, instead of shying away from the situation, internalizing what has happened, or going into a state of denial and avoidance, we can accept our struggles and embrace the saying, "It is what it is!" Honesty goes a long way.

10. Say what you're hoping to get out of telling your person.

There's absolutely nothing wrong with setting expectations. Instead of leaving your chosen person in the dark wondering why you are coming to them, communicate how you think they can help. Explain *why* you chose them.

11. Be brave and go for it!

At some point, there comes a time when we simply need to buckle down and get it done. Keeping things bottled up inside never amounts to great outcomes, and will likely only cause greater suffering down the road. Let us deal with our feelings and emotions right now. Today. Choose communication over silence, and see the great new places it takes you.

> Don't keep all your feelings sheltered—express them. Don't ever let life shut you up.
> ~ **Dr. Steve Maraboli**

FEEL

Whatever you're feeling, tell yourself over and over again: IT'S OKAY.

LEARN

Talking is therapeutic. As human beings, we have an instinctual need to communicate, even if we think we don't. By exercising one of our most powerful tools, we can bring ourselves relief, fresh solutions, happiness and a sense of wellbeing.

DO

Determine who your trusted people are. If something is bothering you or weighing you down, it's time to choose the right person to talk to about that piece of information. Avoid bottling things up—action right away is key.

10
MAKING A CHANGE

> *Although he didn't know it, the bullied boy in the schoolyard that day changed something within me. Our lives had collided—unexpectedly and yet ever so importantly. For the first time in months, I felt a tiny bit like me again. My body felt more alive. Somehow, someway, I had shared Rebecca's story with complete strangers, shameful secrets and all.*
>
> *As terrible a truth as I held inside until that day, I felt liberated to have finally told someone...anyone. Rebecca's story was powerful. I told Rebecca's story to show them, to prove to them, that sometimes it doesn't just go away. Sometimes the bullies don't stop. Sometimes awful things happen, and to prevent them, we must take a stand—as victims, as bystanders, as friends, as teachers, as principals, as parents...as strangers. What if maybe, just maybe, what I did today saved that boy in the schoolyard from years of future torment and misery? What if it inspired the receptionist and principal to begin an anti-bullying initiative at the school to inform and protect their students? If the story and my choice to speak up had the power to make even the smallest impact today, right here and right now, on a single young boy, on a single school—then why couldn't it do the same for other schools full of students?*
>
> **~ Chapter 18, *The Only Way Out***

In the excerpt above, the reader of the novel, *The Only Way Out*, is invited into the internal dialogue of a character who reaches a moment of clarity in her life. She comes to realize that her silence has worked against her, and once she breaks it to speak up about how her friend was bullied and victimized, she feels overwhelmingly free. This character sees how her words can help people.

10. Making a Change

DISCUSSION QUESTIONS

TAKE A MOMENT
Think of the transformation.

1. Describe what feelings, emotions and realizations are happening in the mind of the main character in this scene.

2. What important realization has she come to?

THINGS TO THINK ABOUT

Change is possible.

1. Change can happen. Things are not set in stone. Situations can be repaired, actions moving forward can be altered, people can be different.

2. Change represents an evolving situation. If we ourselves change, this can be a sign of our deepened understanding, our new perspectives, or our personal growth as people.

PERSPECTIVE AND PERCEPTION

People's perceptions and perspectives can differ from one another. Perception is how we use our senses to become aware of something and the ways in which we regard, understand or interpret. The way you perceive a situation might be entirely different from the way your friend, teacher or parent does.

> There is nothing either good or bad, but thinking makes it so.
> ~ **Hamlet, Act II, Scene 2, William Shakespeare**

Perspective is a particular attitude towards something or how we regard it—in other words, our point of view. Our perspective on a specific circumstance can be positive or negative, favorable or unfavorable. We might shrug it off as no big deal, or let it ruin our day. Again, the perspective we take might not be the same as the perspectives of the people around us on the exact same thing.

Negative perceptions and perspectives can lead to negative responses. If, on the other hand, we adopt a more positive and productive understanding and attitude towards the people, things and situations in our lives, we set ourselves up for more successful outcomes.

REWIND, BE KIND

Did you know that before live streaming and DVDs, there were video cassettes? This is how people watched movies prior to the days of Netflix, AppleTV and Amazon Prime. You had to walk or drive to the video rental store, browse the shelves and pick out the video cassette you were interested in watching that night.

On each and every one of the videos in any given video rental store, there was always a sticker.

10. Making a Change

Here's what it said:

BE KIND.
REWIND.

The sticker was asking people to rewind the video cassette tape *before* returning it to the rental store. This required you to leave the video tape in your VCR after you were finished watching it, pressing "rewind" and waiting about two minutes for the rewind process to be completed. This was an act of kindness at the video store because this way, the next customer who paid to rent that video tape wasn't stuck rewinding the video before watching it.

Let's reverse the sticker.

If we were to do that, it would say:

REWIND.
BE KIND.

This new, slightly revised sticker is also asking people to do something important.

It's asking us to rewind a situation. A circumstance. A thing we said. An action we took.

Instead of ignoring a person, walking away, saying the nasty comment or doing something inconsiderate, the sticker prompts us to ask ourselves, what could we have done to be KIND?

Could we have at least flashed a smile to a random, younger student in the hall?
Could we have stood up to the person who picked on our friend?
Could we have given someone a compliment?
Could we have refrained from posting the embarrassing picture of a classmate on social media?

When you take a second to think about any one of these acts of kindness, they seem so simple.

Sure, why couldn't we do that?
No problem.

But there is a problem. The problem is, often we don't.

We choose cruelty over kindness.

But! Kindness is the clear winner in so many ways.

Here's how—and there are real studies to prove it.

Acting kind…

- Releases feel-good hormones, specifically serotonin
- Eases your anxiety
- Reduces stress
- Opens the door to new friendships and strengthens existing ones
- Makes YOU happier when you do it
- Might just make someone else's day

Choosing to be kind is <u>one part</u> of the solution to squash alarmingly high rates of bullying and mental health issues that plague so many of our young people today.

If we personally have a pattern of acting badly, REWIND, BE KIND is an invitation to start thinking differently. After we do this a number of times, there will come a day when we don't need to do the REWIND part. BE KIND will come naturally, and immediately.

If there was more kindness and less cruelty, we would have fewer bullied victims, a decreased number of unhappy youth and young adults, less insecurity and a lower incidence of threatening behaviors towards ourselves and others.

10. Making a Change

BE KIND TO *YOURSELF*

> *Slow and robotic, I forced myself to walk. In that moment, I experienced the crippling sensation of my most haunting, recurrent dream. The one in which I needed desperately to run fast but it was as though a force much greater held me back. I could feel my face wincing in pain and frustration as I tried to be quick. But the fear was too great. It overtook me and my entire body began to shake. In one moment, I heard the screams—the panic—among the students and teachers who stood above her, and in the next, nothing but my own deep, panting breath.*
>
> *....*
>
> *A large lump formed in my throat. I tried to swallow it away but it wouldn't budge, making my breath quicken to a pace that began to terrify me. I was losing control.*
> *Step. I tried to instruct my legs to move.*
> *Step. I tried again.*
> *Gasping for breath, body shaking, knees buckling, somehow I made it. I reached that tainted spot on the field. Stopping dead in my tracks, I stared at the ground beneath my feet.*
>
> **~ Chapter 1, *The Only Way Out***

There are several defense responses to trauma. Two of the most commonly known are "fight" and "flight." These are instinctive physiological responses to threatening situations where we quickly decide either to resist and "fight back" or run away and "take flight."

If we cannot effectively resist or run, another response can take place—the "freeze" response. This is a state of paralysis, much like the one described in the book scene above. Key signs of a freeze response include:

- Increased heart rate
- Shallow, rapid breath
- Hyper alertness
- Built-up energy that cannot be released
- Minimal verbal cues, or no speech at all

- Tension in the body and muscles (tonic immobility, which is an unmoving state in response to extreme fear)

(Source: NICABM)

We can do our best to avoid our body's natural freeze response in a traumatic or fearful situation by first making ourselves aware in advance, of the possibility of it occurring. If we know it exists and we know it can happen, we can handle it better in the moment.

If we are able to recognize the fact that we're having a freeze response, or if we see anyone in this state, psychologists state that the best approach is to take deep breaths, do slow and deep breathing exercises, look around and be aware of the surroundings, and when ready, stand up and move around to loosen the muscles.

It's important to remember that we are all human. Sometimes our reactions to situations are primal, instinctual and physiological, therefore making them beyond our control. We must be kind to ourselves and accept that survival responses are human nature. Care and delicacy are crucial in these fragile states.

Once we are out of the response, then we can redirect our focus to what we should do next.

WE CAN

Change is possible. It always is. In the vast majority of situations, the only thing holding us back from meaningful change is the *want*—and in cases where more than one person is involved, *the collective want*.

In our own personal mental health, we must have a *want* for happiness. A want for peace.

In our treatment of those around us, we must have a *want* for fairness. A want for equality.

If we can establish this want among us, then we can take the next steps towards producing the change.

10. Making a Change

We CAN respect others.
We CAN respect ourselves.
We CAN consider people's feelings.
We CAN be there for another person when they need it.
We CAN be there for ourselves when we're struggling.
We CAN choose kindness over cruelty.
We CAN speak up.
We CAN be different.
We CAN break the cycle.

Take a few minutes to make your own ANTIBULLYING acrostic. An acrostic is a poem or composition of words where each letter of one word starts a new line, spelling out a new word or message. Make your acrostic motivating, inspiring and actionable. For example, the first A might spell out the word "Act." The second letter, N, might stand for "No, is what you say when you're standing up for yourself or someone else." And so on.

Give it a try.

A ....
N ....
T ....
I ....
B ....
U ....
L ....
L ....
Y ....
I ....
N ....
G ....

MOVING FORWARD

Open dialogue and conversation around the pertinent topics of bullying and mental health are even more important than rewinding and being kind. We now know and acknowledge that talking openly and speaking up are often two of the hardest things for us to do. Whether we've seen something, experienced something, or are currently going through a challenge in our own life, communicating it can be one of the most difficult things we'll ever have to do.

However, if we can start doing it and continue doing it, then it will become a natural part of our everyday lives.

Just as the more we run on the treadmill the greater our endurance, or the more we lift weights the stronger our muscles … the more we talk, the easier it is keep up the dialogue and maintain that productive openness.

It will become a new habit.
It will become second nature.
It will become clear *why* we're doing it (likely in more ways than one).
It will become something we want to do (not something we force ourselves to do).

Take a few minutes to make a flag. Your flag can be anything you want it to be. Think about concepts that revolve around kindness, togetherness, happiness, and talking openly and speaking up. Draw and color your flag below, and then feel free to cut it out and paste it on a stick.

10. Making a Change

Your flag:

ACTIONABLE TASKS

As we approach the end of our journey together in this book, there are only two important actionable tasks to leave you with.

1. Want it.

Allow yourself to want a change. Be it in your life, or someone else's, the solution can start with you. After all, it has to start somewhere.

Write down the first three things that come to mind that you are unhappy or dissatisfied with in your life. Pay particular attention to those that affect you or someone else mentally, physically or emotionally.

For example:

> "I don't like my teacher."
> "My friend makes me feel stupid."
> "Piano is too hard."
> "I always get hurt at hockey."
> "My parents are never home."
> "I'm always comparing myself to my friends."
> "My wardrobe sucks."
> "My friend gets bullied."
> "A student in my class always seems unhappy."

1. _____

2. _____

3. _____

In your mind and body, feel the strong want that you have for something to change. Sit with that feeling.

And then...

2. Follow through.

It's time to act. What good is a strong feeling if that's only as far as it goes? Feelings are meant to ignite action. Let us not wallow in our feelings and emotions to the point where we spend our time thinking and complaining about the things we're deeply dissatisfied with. If we do this, we're stuck in step 1 and we never make it to step 2. There is more to be done.

First, we must feel, then we must follow through.

Make a plan. Think of who you can talk to. Figure out where to start.

10. Making a Change

Write down one idea you have to improve or solve each item on your list above.

1. _____

2. _____

3. _____

Then, go. Begin. Get moving in a positive direction.

This attitude and action are what will enable you, and the people around you, to live your best lives.

> Change is never easy, but always possible.
> **~ Barack Obama**

FEEL

Come to terms with the good and the bad in your life. Accept the feelings that come along with doing that.

LEARN

Ask yourself why you feel the way you do about different parts of your life. Evaluate how strong those feelings are and whether or not they require your attention and action. Is change needed? If so, it's time to <u>want</u> it.

DO

You cannot control what others say or do, but you can control what YOU say and do. Be the start of a positive change. Make small steps towards improving a part of your life, or the life of someone else. Find the kindness within you and share it. It begins with you.

> If we can create a home, classroom, environment and culture where people can speak up and talk openly, and know they are accepted for what they have to say, then the possibilities for positive change are endless.
>
> **~ Katie Kuperman, Author**

NEVER HESITATE TO GET HELP

If ever you or someone you know is in need, and you feel as though you have no one to call on for help, turn to your community resources. There is <u>always</u> someone you can find to help you.

In the case of an emergency or crisis situation:

- Call 911
- Visit the closest emergency department in your area

In a case where you need someone to talk to immediately:

- Local Fire Department
- Closest Police Station or Police Service
- Community Distress Center
- Kids Help Phone
- Crisis and Mental Health Lines

National Canadian Help Lines:

- Wellness Together Canada—1.888.668.6810 or text WELLNESS to 686868
- First Nations Hope for Wellness Help Line—1.855.242.3310
- Kids Help Phone—1.800.668.6868
- BullyingCanada Lifeline Support Network—1.877.352.4497 Call or Text

National United States Help Lines:

- National Parent Helpline—1.855.427.2736
- Suicide Prevention Lifeline—1.800.273.8255
- Mental Health Services—1.800.662.4357

REFERENCES

unesco.org
statcan.gc.ca
psychologytoday.com
aplatformforgood.org
stopbullying.gov
betterhelp.com
security.org
cyberbullying.org
ditchthelabel.org
ncpc.org
reviewlution.ca
publicsafety.gc.ca
news.uga.edu
unicef.org
nicabm.com
stompoutbullying.org
apa.org
cpa.ca

www.ingramcontent.com/pod-product-compliance
Lightning Source LLC
Chambersburg PA
CBHW081619100526
44590CB00021B/3508